Joy in Worship

Understanding Worship
According to the Word of God

James Vickery

Joy in Worship

Copyright © 2010 by James Vickery

All rights reserved. No part of this book may be reproduced or transmitted in any form or by any means without written permission of the author.

Unless otherwise noted Scripture is taken from the New King James Version. Copyright © 1979, 1980, 1982 by Thomas Nelson, Inc. Used by permission. All rights reserved.

Published by: Theocentric Publishing Group
                1069 Main St.
                Chipley, FL 32428

www.theocentricpublishing.com

ISBN 9780984570843

I dedicate this book to the many congregations I have served through the years. To those who still reside in this life and the many who are now with the Lord, it was and is my pleasure to share the precious Word of God. I'm grateful God's grace is sufficient to take me as I am and use the things He has blessed me with for His glory!

Foreword

Joy in Worship has become a good friend to me. Reading the manuscript several times has given me a new perspective on worship.

This book is intellectually stimulating and emotionally exhilarating. The Word of God is the foundation upon which this book communicates the principles of biblical worship. Like the roots of a tree provide nourishment for the entire life of the tree, the nourishment for this book comes from the Word of God.

Growing to maturity will always find challenges that may seem contrary to what one has believed in the past. You will probably be challenged as you read this book. For instance, if you've always "gone to church" you will be challenged to "go to worship." The simplicity of assembling for worship is at the same time the profundity of biblical truth.

The centrality of the Word of the God is prominent throughout the book. Although there are many scriptural references, the exposition of the Psalms of Ascent (Psalms 120-134) is unique. They show the passions and reality of the life of the worshiper. You will be drawn in the worship experience of the Old Testament worshipers. You will feel their sorrow in the valley and their joy on the mountain. Behold the wonder of worshiping in unity with those of like precious faith

Martin Murphy, Author and Publisher

Table of Contents

1. Born to Worship 1
2. Biblical Principles of Worship 9
3. The Sordid Faces of False Worship 17
4. The Prominence of True Worship 25
5. A Special Place to Meet God 33
6. God's People Desire True Worship 39
7. Sanctified for Worship 45
8. The Church Assembles for Worship 51
9. The Mercy of God in Worship 57
10. The Guardian of the Church 65
11. Security for the Redeemed Worshiper 73
12. Preparation for Heavenly Worship 81
13. Worship by Divine Favor 89
14. Fear and Blessing in Worship 95
15. The Redeemed Suffering Church 101
16. The Redeemed Worshiping Church 109
17. God is the Center of Worship 117
18. Worship Coram Deo 123
19. Worship is Like Heaven on Earth 131
20. Double Blessing in Worship 137
21. How to Offer Perfect Worship 143

22. The Benediction 149

1. Born to Worship

Psalm 95

The great German theologian, Karl Barth, said, "worship is the most momentous, the most urgent, the most glorious action that can take place in human life!" (Karl Barth, quoted in J. J. Allman, *Worship: It's Theology and Practice*, p. 133). Although Barth may not be your favorite theologian, his statement on worship is truth down to every syllable.

Worship is an innate principle that belongs to God's rational creatures and more specifically the human race. Worship constitutes an inborn principle expressed by the thoughts and actions of the worshiper. Worship is either introverted or extroverted. Worship as a principle of life begins with the first breath and will continue eternally. Introverted worship is self worship. Extroverted worship is worship of some object beyond self.

If you belong to God because of the sacrifice of Christ on your behalf and applied by the power of the Holy Spirit, you will have a unique worship experience.

We are all creatures of habit. Sometimes we just take something for granted because it is just part of life. For instance, worship may become the hour long event on Sunday mornings that most Christians refer to as "going to church." Since worship is natural to all people it would be presumptuous to assume the level of understanding from the individual perspective. It is wise to review some of the basics relative to Christian worship.

It has been said that the great football coach Vince Lombardi began every new season with a lecture on the basics of football. He literally held up a football and said, "This is a football." He talked about its size and shape, how it can be kicked, carried, or passed.

Figuratively speaking, I hold up the word "worship." Although it is not a difficult word to pronounce, it probably has a wide range of meanings in the American culture. It is derived from two old English words that are very familiar. The first word is "worth." It refers to something of excellence, something of value, or the quality of goodness. The next part of the word that constructs the word worship is "ship." It is a noun forming suffix that denotes a state of condition or describes the quality of the attached word. For example, there are words like friendship that describe the quality of two people in a relationship. The word authorship defines a quality attributed to the author of a literary work.

Christians must go a step further to understand the meaning of the word worship. The Word of God is their source to understand the biblical concept commonly called worship.

The Old Testament has three words that will help Christians understand the meaning of the English word "worship." The first Hebrew word translated into English is *shachah*. The primary meaning is "bow down." It is also translated into English as homage, prostrate, and worship. The Hebrew word *qadad* is also translated worship. The primary meaning is "bow down [low]." Since the Bible was eventually translated into the Greek language, it is necessary to examine the Greek words for worship. The concept of worship is traced to the Greek word *gonu*. The primary meaning refers to the body part known as "the knee." The Greek word *proskuneo* is a close relative of the English word worship. Its basic meaning is "to do reverence." Some Bible scholars connect *proskuneo* to the word "kiss". It was common in the Greek culture to kiss the earth to do reverence to the false gods of the earth. The Hebrew word *abad* and the Greek word *latreuo*, both have the primary meaning "to serve." To worship God and to serve God are inseparably connected and in some sense they are synonymous. Although there are many nuances to these words, they are sufficient to have a basic understanding of biblical worship.

Born to Worship

Genesis chapter twenty-four is the inspired story of Abraham sending his trusted servant to find Isaac a wife. Both of these Hebrew words translated into English are found in that text. When the servant found God's choice for Isaac he "bowed his head" and "worshiped the LORD" (Genesis 24:48). The bodily gesture of submitting in humility before God is related to the very idea of worship. The outward gesture expressing humility must come from a humble heart before God.

God communicates to His children with words that are rational, but they also connect to inward sensations. To put that in everyday language, God's people ought to have an emotional response to His rational words. God chose the words "bow down" as a gesture to worship Him. The symbolical nature of bowing down calls for humility. Standing before the judgment seat of Christ will be the most public display of the human race. "For it is written: As I live, says the LORD, Every knee shall bow to Me, And every tongue shall confess to God" (Romans 14:11).

The bending of the knee, bowing down, or to lay face down on the ground are manifestations of an inward sense of man's place before God. It represents humility in the presence of God showing a submissive and loving disposition toward God. The gestures one makes in worship will indicate the adoration, reverence, and respect for the object of worship.

If Christians do not understand the object of worship, then the concept of worship is worthless. For most Americans the object of worship is an idol. There is a very popular television show called "American Idol." The records will show that roughly twenty five million Americans look at that show. *Webster's Dictionary* defines an idol as an "image, material object, person, thing, a figment of the mind, a fantasy, or a false conception of something." Webster goes on to define an idol as "any person or thing devotedly or excessively admired." So an American Idol is someone that receives excessive admiration. This nation will regret making the "American Idol" the object of worship.

Satan tempted Jesus Christ, the second person of the Trinity, God in the flesh, with objects of this world, but Jesus said "You shall worship the LORD your God, and Him only you shall serve" (Matthew 4:10).

Christians have one object of worship. He is the Lord your God. Ralph Martin, a New Testament scholar and theologian, once said, "the goal of worship is the adoration of God for His own sake."

One of the fundamental principles of Christian worship is the antepenultimate object. He is God. It may sound sophomoric but the basis for worship is found in these four words: "In the beginning God..." (Genesis 1:1). If that sounds juvenile, then the question to ask is, "why is there so much false worship in the world?"

The one basic necessity of worship is to know the object of worship. A few of God's attributes will help Christians grasp His nature and character.

> God is pure spirit. Exponentially multiplied worth belongs to God because of His unique spiritual nature. Contrary to the belief of some world religions, God is not visible and has no body parts. For instance The Church of the Latter Day Saints believes that "The Father has a body of flesh and bones as tangible as man" (*The Doctrine and Covenants* 130:3). (See John 4:24 for the biblical doctrine).

> God is omnipresent. He is everywhere present at one time. Therefore worship may be offered anytime and any place. (Psalm 139:7)

> God is omniscient. He knows everything that was, is, or ever will be. God's knowledge is full knowledge. He knows the heart and knows if worship is offered for His own sake. (1 John 3:20)

God is omnipotent. He is all-powerful and will defend the powerless, so they may offer true worship to the only living and true God. (Luke 1:37)

An intellectual and emotional understanding of your object of worship is not enough. There must be a unique and personal relationship with the worshiper and the object of worship. Satan has an intellectual apprehension of God, but Satan does not offer any worthiness to God (James 2:19). Satan does not have a good relationship with God. To cry out with an emotional response, without a true knowledge of God and motivation to worship God is mockery (Hosea 8:2). The intellect and the emotions are involved in worship, but they must be in a relationship with God.

God reveals Himself in the most unique way. God is transcendent in His relationship with those who worship Him. God is distinctly different than anything in this world or in the mind of man. To use an old fashioned seldom used term, God is incomprehensible (Psalm 145:3). God is above and apart from any earthly power. All of the government agencies, educational institutions, scientific advances and religious organizations are infinitesimally worthless compared to the transcendent God of exponential worth.

The uniqueness of God's relationship with His creation is that His transcendence does not diminish His immanence. God is immanent in the lives of Christians in a very special way (Isaiah 57:15). The relational oneness that God has with His child is not merely way off in eternity. "For indeed, the kingdom of God is within you" is not wishful thinking (Luke 17:21).

God is spirit, eternal, independent, and incomprehensible thus He is transcendent. God is within your reach which is evident from His providence and His redemptive activity. The privilege of knowing God in this unique sense should cause every Christian to worship Him with all the faculties of body and soul. The more Christians examine the basics of biblical worship, the more they will find that God established the relationship "in the beginning." God created and invested in mankind the natural inclination to worship.

The inclination of man to worship God is inseparable from God's injunction that requires worship. The Psalmist explains the doctrine in these terms:

> The injunction from God is "come."
> The inclination is "let us worship."
> The inclination is "let us bow down."
> The inclination is "let us kneel."
> (Psalm 95:6)

God's command and the passion of the worshiper describe the reality of dignity, awe, respect, and love all wrapped up in one experience. It is the experience of being willing and able to worship before the face of Jehovah, the Lord God almighty. It is an experience that brings the dignity, majesty, and worth of the Lord God our Maker into a public, but personal relationship.

There are reasons beyond enumerating for the child of God to worship the Father. There are a few basic reasons found in the inspired Word of God in Psalm ninety-five.

The Psalm refers to God's creative power and His love for the creature (Psalm 95:5). He made the sea and formed the land for the benefit of His special creation: you. How do you worship the One that gives life? Humbly you bow down low and look up high to see the face of the Lord God, your maker.

God's providential care is another reason for Christians to worship God. God provides everything for life. God is independent, but He is generous and supplies all the needs of a dependent creation. Do you find pleasure in offering praise and thanksgiving for God's generous provision to you?

The Bible gives another reason to worship; God is great. The recognition of God's greatness comes from His creative power and providential care. God's greatness has no boundaries, but reveals His immensity. In His systematic theology, Dr. Morton Smith writes, "[Immensity] means that he is above all of creation" (*Systematic Theology*, Dr. Morton Smith, vol. 1, p. 135). Solomon understood the greatness of God which is revealed in his prayer of dedication of the temple. Solomon said, "Behold, heaven and the heaven of heavens cannot contain You" (1 Kings 8:27).

The most humbling reason to worship the Lord is particularly important to those people redeemed by God's saving grace. He is "the Rock of our salvation." The Rock is Jesus Christ (1 Corinthians 10:1-4). Jesus Christ is not merely the source of salvation, He is the salvation for all who believe (John 3:36). Those who belong to God because of the finished work of Jesus Christ and redeemed by the power of the Holy Spirit will have a burning passion to worship the "Rock of our salvation."

A.W. Tozer tells the story of his visit to an old building in Mexico. While he was there a Mexican woman came in and went straight to the altar area. It seemed as if she could have walked there with her eyes closed. She kneeled directly in front of a statue of the virgin Mary. She looked at that statue with a sense of deep devotion, deep yearning, and deep desire. There she poured out her worship on a lifeless statue which was the work of a person's hand. (See the entire story in *Whatever Happened to Worship*, A. W. Tozer, chapter 3)

She probably did not understand that she was born to worship the true and living God. Somewhere along the way, she failed to understand the basic principles of Christian worship. She failed to have an awareness of God's glory and His worthiness to receive her worship. She was emotionally involved in worship, but in reality there was no intellectual connection.

This is the invitation to Christians everywhere! Go back to the basics for worship and by the grace of God you will come to the same conclusion as Karl Barth. "Worship is the most momentous, the most urgent, the most glorious action that can take place in human life!

2. Biblical Principles of Worship

Isaiah 6:1-3

Demas looked into his mother's eyes with despair in his eyes. "Mom, do I have to go to church today." The request from the six year old child was touching, but the answer was not "no or yes." "Demas, you will have fun in children's church," was the answer. The stern male voice down the hall overwhelmed the emotional plea. "Hurry up, we'll be late for church!"

Does this conversation sound familiar or at least something similar to it? If you planned to go to a football game would you tell people you were going to a basketball game? Unless you purposely intend to deceive someone the answer is probably "no." Why do Christians say, "I'm going to church" or "let's go to church" or some similar phraseology about attending church?

Since all individual believers constitute the church, it is impossible for the church to go to church. The church may gather or assemble for a variety of reasons including Bible study, fellowship, prayer, or worship. Christians do not and cannot go to church. The church can and should go to worship.

The good news is that the children of God constitute the church. The other good news is that God calls all His children to worship Him. His children were born to worship. Since God is good and gracious, He preserved the principles of worship for His children. The great St. Augustine of Hippo was in misery trying to understand the meaning of life. In a mysterious way Augustine heard the voice of a child saying *"tolle lege."* It is a Latin phrase that means "take up and read." Christians must *tolle lege* the Bible to understand the principles of worship. The arch principle is "the church worships God in spirit and truth" (John 4:24). Return to basic Christian doctrine and say, "the church assembles to worship." Break the bad habit of saying "let's go to church." On Sunday morning say, "today is the Lord's Day and the church must assemble to worship. I'm part of the church, so I'm going to worship."

The doctrine of worship is probably the most neglected doctrine among evangelicals. There are plenty of books and discussion on worship. However, there is a serious lack of teaching the doctrine of worship from a biblical perspective.

It is not possible to grasp the full meaning of worship until Christians grasp the full counsel of God. Have you ever tried to assemble something without reading all the instructions first? It is eternally important to read the whole Bible and bring it together systematically to better understand the doctrine of worship. The principles of worship are derived from the full counsel of God.

God established a perfect plan and gave it to His perfect creation before sin entered into the world. His perfect plan was explained in terms of three fundamental principles which are found in the second chapter of Genesis. Christians must be careful at this point because God ordered these pre-fall mandates before sin entered into the world. God gave them to a world without sin and to the two sinless federal representatives of the human race.

Christians must not ignore these creational ordinances. There are a number of interpretational theories about these ordinances. One school of thought is that they were abrogated or grossly modified at the fall. Another school of thought is that they are perpetual and therefore apply to the entire human race, both believers and unbelievers. It is possible to let each principle stand on its own merit, but consequences may lead to a dead end with serious contradiction.

The first is the Sabbath principle (Genesis 2:1-3). The Sabbath principle is rooted in God's covenant promise to give His people rest. It does not mean God turns people into couch potatoes. It is the time to be refreshed in the special presence of God. Some people refuse to be refreshed by God's special presence even though God's "eternal power and Godhead" is evident. For that reason the Sabbath principle is further defined in the moral law (Exodus 20:8-11).

The Sabbath principle is the special occasion for God's people to rest from their individual and family worship and join the company of believers to "call upon the Lord who is worthy to be praised" (Psalm 18:3). Although the Sabbath principle is a unique expression of Worship to God, the principle is timeless. "Trust in Him at all times, you people; Pour out your heart before Him" (Psalm 62:8). Although God gave specific and perfect instructions as to how "the company of believers" must worship, it will never be perfect in a sinful world. This dimension of worship will be perfected in Heaven.

The Sabbath principle magnified by the presence of the Lord God of heaven and earth becomes the theater for the universality of public worship. The absence of instruction relative to this doctrine has caused immeasurable suppression of what otherwise may have been the uniting of God's people for worship.

The prophet Isaiah had a unique experience that magnifies worship principles.

> In the year that King Uzziah died, I saw the Lord sitting on a throne, high and lifted up, and the train of His robe filled the temple. Above it stood seraphim; each one had six wings; with two he covered his face, with two he covered his feet, and with two he flew. And one cried to another and said: "Holy, holy, holy is the Lord of hosts; The whole earth is full of His glory!" (Isaiah 6:1-3)

It is necessary to introduce the word *theophany* to better understand the text in Isaiah. A *theophany* is a combination of two Greek words; *theos* referring to God and *phaneros* referring to appearance. Therefore, a *theophany* is a manifestation of God. For example Moses had a theophany with the burning bush (Exodus 3:2-6). Isaiah had a theophany of God either through a vision or a mysterious translation. In either case Isaiah "saw the Lord." Isaiah experienced a theophany that every Christian ought to desire to understand rationally and feel it emotionally.

The angel spoke to Isaiah and said," Holy, holy, holy is the Lord of hosts; The whole earth is full of His glory" (Isaiah 6:3). This ought to jump out of your heart and mind and scream to the whole world. The whole earth manifests the presence of God. Do you understand God's presence? Do you experience God's presence? The words of the angel indicate the universal public nature of worship. All of the pomp, ceremony, and religious solemnities will not substitute for the exercise of the Sabbath principle.

The Sabbath principle is innate and any attempt to denigrate its reality will destroy the substance of society. A few inspired examples from God's mouth are sufficient to remind His people of this important principle.

> In those days I saw people in Judah treading wine presses on the Sabbath, and bringing in sheaves, and loading donkeys with wine, grapes, figs, and all kinds of burdens, which they brought into Jerusalem on the Sabbath day. And I warned them about the day on which they were selling provisions. Men of Tyre dwelt there also, who brought in fish and all kinds of goods, and sold them on the Sabbath to the children of Judah, and in Jerusalem. Then I contended with the nobles of Judah, and said to them, 'What evil thing is this that you do, by which you profane the Sabbath day? Did not your fathers do thus, and did not our God bring all this disaster on us and on this city? Yet you bring added wrath on Israel by profaning the Sabbath. (Nehemiah 13:15-18)

This text reveals the condition of the Old Testament congregation after they returned to rebuild the walls of the city and the temple in Jerusalem. They had spent seventy years in exile and you would think they would be careful to obey God. Nehemiah's question should provoke the heart of every Christian. "Did not your fathers do thus, and did not our God bring all this disaster on us and on this city?" They forgot the Sabbath principle. They forgot that the holiness of God and the full manifestation of His glory.

Jesus clarifies any ambiguity about the relationship that man has with the Sabbath. Jesus said to the Jewish religious leaders, "The Sabbath was made for man, and not man for the Sabbath" (Mark 2:27).

God included the Sabbath principle in the religious, social and political life of His congregation in the Old Testament (Leviticus 23:3). The Lord promises His blessing on those who keep the Sabbath principle (Exodus 20:11). The joy in the Sabbath principle will be expressed in the faithfulness of the worshiper (Psalm 40:10).

The second creational ordinance is the family principle (Genesis 2:18-25). The familial relation established before the fall is a universal enduring principle. "Therefore a man shall leave his father and mother and be joined to his wife, and they shall become one flesh" (Genesis 2:24). The husband/wife relation is built on three principles: Leave, cleave, and become one. God's covenant relationship extends to the offspring of this union. "Be fruitful and multiply; fill the earth and subdue it" is the cultural mandate given to the family (Genesis 1:28).

God established the family to worship together. God promised to bless the families that belong to the family of God (Genesis 12:3). Since worship is natural to mankind, the family as an institution has the distinct responsibility and privilege to worship the Creator of the family. It is a great duty God has given to the father, joined with his wife, to teach the progeny to worship the Lord (Deuteronomy 6:4-9).

The family is the basic institution of God's kingdom on earth. It is the spiritual strength of the families that make up the church of Jesus Christ. Joshua, the son of Nun, told the whole company of families of Israel that he and his family would serve the Lord (Joshua 24:15). Joshua acknowledged God's supremacy, he put away false gods, and assumed the role of leadership. To serve the Lord is to worship the Lord, so Joshua's family could worship the Lord and say, "Holy, holy, holy is the Lord of hosts"

In 1647 the Westminster Assembly published the *Directions for Family Worship*. Among those directions we find these instructions: "These exercises [family worship] ought to be performed in great sincerity, without delay, laying aside all exercises of worldly business or hinderances, notwithstanding the mocking of atheists and profane men." The godly men who wrote these directions simply believed it was normal for families to engage in worship (Acts 5:42).

The third creational ordinance is service in a secular world (Genesis 2:15; 1:26-30). Some theologians call it the work ethic, but "work" is too narrow a definition for this principle found in Scripture. God told the perfect people in a perfect place to "subdue" it. In the modern world, the word "subdue" probably raises the idea of bringing something or someone under control of someone else. However, not to be redundant, but God could not possibly mean for Adam to captivate anyone or anything, because it was a perfect world. In the context of a perfect world, Adam had the responsibility to mirror the "image of God" before all of creation. Since Adam was the federal representative for the human race, this concept applies to everyone, not just Christians.

To replicate the image of God means to think like God according to His rational gifts which include logic, knowledge, and wisdom. It also means to make decisions that line up with God's moral law. God gave man a mind and will. The capstone to the image of God is the way man expresses his mind and will. In modern language it is called the emotions. In times past godly men referred to it as the "affections" of man. I personally like the word "affections" relative to the expressions of the soul, because an affectionate personality reflects the mercy and grace of God.

The word emotions often refers to negativity and anger as much as it does love and compassion.

God gave this unique person a mandate that applies to every human being. Every individual on this planet, has the honor and joy of "tending" to God's garden. The word "tend" in the New King James Version comes from the Hebrew word *abad*. The word *abad* essentially means "to serve." Adam was given three creational ordinances: Sabbath, family, and serving in God's kingdom on earth. A better understanding of these ordinances will enhance your understanding of worship. Until Adam introduced sin into the world, his whole life consisted of worship to God.

It is true that we do not live in a perfect world and we are not perfect people. The fall and introduction of sin into the world did not destroy the image of God in man, it just defaced it. For those who belong to Jesus Christ the image has been renewed. Not perfected, although it will be when our bodies are glorified before God.

The renewed image in man cries out to God in worship. First as an individual we worship God in all our work (Exodus 20:9). Christians ought to observe from that text that it is a commandment: go labor and work for six days. The word "labor" comes from the Hebrew word *abad* also refers to service. The word "work" comes from the Hebrew word *melakah* meaning to engage in some productive craft or project. Serving God by using the gifts that God has given, is the glory of worship.

The image of God will shine through the soul of God's children when they worship Him. The child of God must not worship the work of his own hands, but rather worship the God who gave the hands for work. The image of God will shine through the soul when the family gathers together and reads the Word of God and prays for God's grace. The image of God will shine through the soul when the church gathers to worship the giver of all gifts. It is important to remember that the soul will eternally worship God.

Religion in the soul of man is dead without the means to worship the supremacy of God the Father, God the Son, and God the Holy Spirit. In your mind visit the scene of the angels as they cried to one another, "Holy, holy, holy is the Lord of Hosts; The whole earth is full of His glory" (Isaiah 6:3). Then Listen to God:

> For thus says the High and Lofty One Who inhabits eternity, whose name is Holy: I dwell in the high and holy place, With him who has a contrite and humble spirit To revive the spirit of the humble, And to revive the heart of the contrite ones. (Isaiah 57:15)

> To live is to worship and say to your God: In Your presence is fullness of joy; At Your right hand are pleasures forevermore. (Psalm 16:11)

3. The Sordid Faces of False Worship

Isaiah 2:8

God created a perfect world. He created perfect people. God was perfect. It was a wonderful world until the crafty old deceiver raised his ugly face. "Indeed has God said?" After the old Devil said, "You surely shall not die!" the trial turned into a temptation (Genesis 2:4). Adam and Eve succumbed to the temptations of Satan. Of course no human being alive today was present to see the chronology of the developments or the instantaneous event. The fleeting breath of the progeny for the human race changed true worship into false worship when Adam and Eve sinned against God. God-centered worship changed to man-centered worship. God-centered worship places God at the center of worship. Man-centered worship places man at the center of worship. The object of worship changed from God to man.

Worship is either true or false. True worship is offered from a saved sinner to God. The heavenly Father accepts worship because of the perfect sacrifice of the Lord Jesus Christ. The Holy Spirit empowers the saved sinner to offer worship acceptable to the Lord. True worship begins with God giving His people His instructions so He will receive the glory from worship.

False worship was evident from the fall of the sinful human race. True worship is acceptable to God; false worship is not acceptable. The story of Cain and Able reveals God's attitude towards true worship and false worship (Genesis 4:3-8).

The worship offered by Cain and Abel is an early form of the principle of the first fruit doctrine. Deuteronomy chapter twenty-six explains the principle of the first fruit offering. Cain's offering was appropriate according to God's generous providence. Some Bible teachers argue that Abel brought a blood sacrifice which was acceptable to God, but God would not accept

Cain's offering. It is a sad commentary that the first worship experience described in the Bible is so easily misinterpreted. Cain's worship, not his offering, was not acceptable to God. It may be deduced from the rest of Scripture that Cain offered God worship from a bad heart. Cain's heart was not right before God and obviously did not love the object of worship.

Cain loved himself and sought the first place in the earthly kingdom. He realized that Abel had a right relationship with God and offered a spiritual sacrifice. Jealousy and envy will tempt the prideful heart to detest true and worthy worship.

God's displeasure towards false worship does not have a good ending. Christians ought to read the account of false worship in Leviticus chapter ten. The Lord gave specific instructions for offering worship relative to the use of fire and incense (Leviticus 16:12). It is clear that God commanded Nadab and Abihu, the worship leaders, to worship a specific way and they offered worship "which He [God] had not commanded them" (Leviticus 10:1-2). Nabad and Abihu were punished most severely for their disobedience in worship.

Generational continuity is necessary to pass along the doctrine, form, and expression of true worship. Failure to teach each generation the principles of godly and true worship will give rise to the ugly faces of false worship.

Eli's sons sinned in the context of worship. Apparently Eli failed to correct them and teach them the proper way to worship God. Furthermore they did not know the Lord (1 Samuel 2:12). Eli should not have allowed them to lead in worship. Eli's failure provoked "the Lord to judge his house forever for the iniquity which he knew, because his sons brought a curse on themselves and he did not rebuke them (1 Samuel 3:13).

Worship offered by wicked people is repulsive to the Lord. Worthless offerings and unsanctified religious assemblies are an abomination to the Lord (Isaiah 1:10-15). False worship comes from a proud heart and a rebellious mind. "Man looks at the outward appearance, but the Lord looks at the heart"

(1Samuel 16:7). The unbeliever's pride of life eschews the grace of God, but treasures the external works of the hands.

The testimony of the Lord Jesus Christ denounces man-made hypocritical worship. His words ought to cause the heart to tremble.

> THIS PEOPLE HONORS ME WITH THEIR LIPS, BUT THEIR HEART IS FAR AWAY FROM ME. BUT IN VAIN DO THEY WORSHIP ME, TEACHING AS DOCTRINES THE PRECEPTS OF MEN. (Matthew 15:8-9)

Jesus leaves no question about the estrangement from God in worship, if man-made doctrine is the standard. It is a heart problem, but the outward expression is vain worship. Man wants to be in control and for that reason he "worships the work of his hands" (Hosea 14:3; Isaiah 2:8).

There are many narrative descriptions of worship in the Old Testament and a less number in the New Testament. The people of God are under the influence of idolatry because of the sinful heart. For that reason God commanded His people not to make an idol (Exodus 20:4). The sin of syncretism relative to worship visits every generation of God's people. Syncretism is the practice of adopting some form or forms of false worship and mixing those forms with the true worship. For instance, the Old Testament congregation worshipped Baal and Jehovah. By the time the prophet Jeremiah came on the scene, the Old Testament congregation seemed to be very comfortable with Baal worship along with true worship.

Syncretism is mixing worship offered to the Creator with worship offered to the creature. Unfortunately some professing Christians gather to worship God, but they also worship the preacher, song leader, choir, building, stained glass windows, or some other created object. But God says, "you shall have no other gods before me" (Exodus 20:2).

The contemporary church ought to pay attention to the narrative found in the book of Jeremiah.

> Thus says the Lord: "Stand in the court of the Lord's house, and speak to all the cities of Judah, which come to worship in the Lord's house, all the words that I command you to speak to them. Do not diminish a word." (Jeremiah 26:2)

This text from Jeremiah records a scene in the life of the Old Testament church that occurred about 2600 years ago. The one thing that the contemporary church has in common with the church of 2600 years ago is worship. The worship practices of the people during the life and ministry of Jeremiah and the church today are similar in principle.

The people of God in the day of Jehoiakim the king of Judah (609-597) came to the Lord's house to worship. When the people gathered to worship, God warned the worshipers: "I will make this house like Shiloh" unless the people turn from their evil ways. The worshipers could not entertain the thought of terminating worship at Jerusalem. The worshipers were outraged and threatened to kill the preacher.

Why did they get mad at the preacher? Apparently because he said, speaking for God of course, "I [God] will make this house like Shiloh." Why was Shiloh so important? Shiloh became a place of worship for the Old Testament worshipers during the conquest under the direction of Joshua some 850 years before the scene in Jeremiah. Shiloh was the place of worship under the priesthood of Eli and his two wicked sons. After the Philistines captured the Ark of the Lord, Shiloh lost its significance and was eventually destroyed about 1050 B.C.

When Jeremiah said "this place" (the temple in Jerusalem - the place where the worshipers were presently standing) will be like Shiloh, the worshipers were real upset. The preacher was tampering with their church and their worship. Attitudes toward worship have not changed much in the past 2600 years. Today the murmuring might be something like, "What do you mean tampering with my church! I was baptized here and I love this building."

Another question that comes to mind is why would God be so harsh toward those people who allegedly came to worship Him? The answer is very simple once we examine the history of worship among the Old Testament worshipers. Isaiah wrote these inspired words before the fall of the Northern Kingdom in 722 B.C. "Their land has also been filled with idols; they worship the work of their hands" (Isaiah 2:8). They worship the work of their hands is equal to self-worship. John Calvin was right when he said, "men are experts at inventing idols" (*Commentary on the Acts of the Apostles'*, Acts 28:6, by John Calvin). People love to worship man-made things. God will not tolerate self-worship. Professing believers invent things to worship which may excite the emotions, but ultimately God will depart and then destruction will be imminent. For instance, when the glory of the Lord departed the Temple in Jerusalem (Ezekiel chapter 10), Jerusalem was sacked and the Temple was destroyed.

In this modern/postmodern age true worship has been replaced by entertainment of every sort. The application of managerial theory and the psychobabble theories are the great enemies of true biblical worship. Today as in the day of Jeremiah, the focus is on the worshiper rather than the object of worship. Professing Christian worshipers seem more interested in entertainment for themselves rather than worshiping the Creator. The church must restore biblical worship and learn to worship God according to His pleasure. It is important to teach children the biblical principles of worship. Generational continuity is so important for the Christian church.

Contemporary church leaders look for ways to make the worshiper comfortable during corporate collective worship. The unique and particular doctrine for worship given by God from His mouth recorded in the word of God, often serves as a source of embarrassment to the contemporary church. However, the Word of God determines the acceptable way to worship God.

The competition is fierce. *Church A* wants to out do *Church B* by having a worship service that will produce a visceral response. *Church A* has three different worship times and almost guarantees that one of them will please just about anyone, except God. *Church B* makes every effort to avoid preaching the Word of God and promises to make the worshiper successful in every area of life.

The church pastor/teacher/minister feels threatened because he must compete with the entertainment industry. In fact, many churches in the United States substitute plays, television programs, and athletic superstars in the place of biblical worship. Books have been written and numerous seminars are conducted to teach local pastors how to retain professing Christians and at the same time attract believers and unbelievers to assemble and worship God. Unfortunately pastors may say, "we are looking for ways to make worship more interesting" when in fact they are looking for ways to make worship more entertaining.

The ugly faces of false worship lurk behind every man-centered world view. There are many world views that provoke false worship. Secularism, humanism, materialism, consumerism, pragmatism, positivism, pluralism, relativism, hedonism, and individualism have a long history of joining Christian worship, not as a worshiper, but the object of worship. The secular is not necessarily evil, but adopting secularism as an object of worship is evil. We are all consumers, but that concept must not become an object of worship. It is not difficult to turn a legitimate discipline of life into a god to worship.

Christians learn the concept and doctrine of Christian worship when they very young. Children tend to follow those in authority over them. If they are taught a false doctrine of worship, they tend to follow it unless the Lord intervenes. Generational continuity is an inescapable principle. If there is no systematic doctrine of worship, each generation tends to adopt a hodgepodge of ideas based on emotional intuitions.

The mission of the church is to make disciples and teach the Word of God (Matthew 28:19-20). If the Word of God is correctly taught, worship will be the most prominent aspect in the life of a Christian. Since the ministry of the church is equipping the saints (Ephesians 4:12), worship ought to be a major part of the instructions for Christians. Worship does take place naturally but without following God's prescription, it will naturally be false worship. People do worship without instruction, but it ends in false worship without following God's prescription.

False worship creeps into the congregation of God's people like a snake in the grass. As he did with our first parents, he will try to convince the professing Christian to worship the creature rather than the creator. The next step is easy. The old deceiver will try to convince Christians that the focus on the worshiper is more important than the object of worship. It is then easy for the worshiper to desire secular entertainment rather than to offer spiritual worship to the God of Heaven and Earth.

God calls His people to ignore the ugly faces of false worship. The Lord Jesus Christ is the Mediator of all true worship. Identify with the unique Savior who gives the believer the privilege to appear before the throne of grace in worship. Pray for the power of the Holy Spirit to enable you to glorify God in all your worship.

4. The Prominence of True Worship

Exodus 20:1-11

Worship reflects the heartbeat of the soul. It is the expression of the soul offering worthiness to the object of worship. Christians have the unique privilege of having an intimate relationship with their most dignified object of worship, the Lord God almighty. God defines His relationship with His people by way of covenant. God makes covenants with His people. The covenants establish parameters to regulate their behavior in the relationship.

God's covenant always includes stipulations; a blessing for keeping covenant and a curse for breaking covenant. One of the most prominent covenants found in Scripture is the covenant of law. More often than not the covenant of law is referred to as the Ten Commandments. The first four of the Ten Commandments are covenantal stipulations that describe the special relationship the creature has with the Creator.

The Ten Commandments came directly from the mouth of God and Scripture even mentions that they were written "by the finger of God" (Deuteronomy 9:10). The emphatic nature of this portion of God's Word ought to be considered with great care and attention. There is a distinction between the Ten Commandments and the covenant of law. The Ten Commandments are natural to all men (Romans 2:14-15). The covenant of law was made for the congregation of God's people (Exodus 20:2).

The covenant of law, found in Exodus chapter twenty, must be studied in its context. God gives His people specific instructions relative to the covenant of law. "Therefore, if you will indeed obey My voice and keep My covenant, then you shall be a special treasure to Me above all people; for all the earth is Mine" (Exodus 19:5). When God said, "keep My covenant" it establishes a relationship based on obedience. Covenant keepers will be called God's "special treasure." This is not a campaign for works salvation. Since sinful man is unable to keep the law perfectly, a Mediator is necessary to satisfy God's wrath. The Mediator is the Lord Jesus Christ who perfectly obeyed the law and kept the covenant for the sake of God's children. In the context of "keep My covenant" the relationship between the worshiper and the object of worship is in view. This text does not teach the atonement, sacrifice, or salvation of the parties in the covenant. Other places in the Bible teach that the work of Jesus Christ binds the covenant with His blood (Hebrews 7:22; 9:26). It is the work of the Mediator, the Lord Jesus Christ that makes worship acceptable to God. The believing soul will then endeavor to keep the covenant with a thankful and humble heart, especially in the worship relationship.

    The covenant of law begins with God identifying Himself as the Savior and Lord of His people. He reveals something about His nature and character. Then God reveals and establishes the injunctions found in the covenant of law. The first three commandments are often called the God-first commandments because they explain the character of God and the nature of the relationship between the parties. They direct our attention to God and His personality.

    The stipulations set forth in the covenant of law positively establish the prominence of true worship. Although it may appear to be negative, it is actually positive for God to instruct the worshiper; "you shall have no other gods before Me" (Exodus 20:3). The one true and living God is the divine majesty over all of heaven and earth, the seen and the unseen. True worship begins with recognizing the supremacy and sovereignty of God over His creation.

    When the Pharisees asked Jesus, "which is the greatest commandment in the law" Jesus responded, "You shall love the Lord your God with all your heart, with all your soul, and with all your mind" (Mt. 22:37). The centrality of God in the presence of His creation is prominent in the hearts of those who love Him.

The passion of the soul is to come into the presence of God with adoration, fascination, wonder, and awe.

> For the Lord is great and greatly to be praised…
> Honor and majesty are before Him;
> Strength and majesty are before Him;
> O worship the Lord in the beauty of holiness.
> (Psalm 96:4-9)

If you have no other gods before the one true and living God then you will worship Him with all of your adoration and trust. Then you will see the prominence of true worship. Then you will find great pleasure in your covenant relationship with Him.

The covenant of law not only gives a definitive explanation relative to the object of worship; it also establishes the parameters for the manner of worship. The second commandment follows from the first in that it explains how to worship the true and living God.

God's instruction is manifestly clear. This commandment specifically removes human autonomy in worship. To put it another way, Christians are not free to establish laws for worship. Christians are free to worship God alone without the assistance of man created objects.

True worship is spiritual. The second commandment is most positive for the Christian because it removes the caricatures of worship. The external ceremonies, pomp, and regalia are not necessary for spiritual worship. The soul recognizes the majesty, splendor, dignity, and beauty of God. True worship is the magnificence of God in the soul of man.

The prominence of true worship is spiritual. God is a spiritual being and Christians must conceive of God spiritually. The only way to know who to worship is by having the spiritual eyes opened. It is the renewing of the mind, emotions and will that allows you to worship the true and living God.

It is not enough to worship the true God. Christians must worship Him truthfully. God requires His children to worship Him in spirit and truth. The Roman philosopher Cicero is credited with this quote. "The best, the purest, the holiest, and the most pious worship of the gods is to worship them with a heart and tongue always pure, upright, and untainted." He was not a Christian, but if he had come under the power of the Holy Spirit, his remark about worship only needed a couple of corrections. Let's change "gods" to "God" and "them" to "Him" and read it again. "The best, the purest, the holiest, and the most pious worship of God is to worship Him with a heart and tongue always pure, upright, and untainted." Two words changed the ugly face of false worship to the prominence of true worship.

Truth adores the nature and character of the Triune God. Christians must be very careful to offer true worship to the true God in the true manner in which He has prescribed in His Word. Christians do not have to figure out what God wants in worship. The Word of God explains that God wants all your attention. He is jealous and will not share His place in worship with anyone or anything. He is jealous of His people, in the right sense of course. They are the apple of His eye. God is jealous because He is sovereign and has the right to rule over His creatures.

The discovery of God's truth relative to worship requires a humble heart and a diligent mind. God requires His church to do all things, including worship, decently and in order for His glory (1 Corinthians 10:31; 14:40). It is necessary to consult the whole counsel of God, the Old and New Testament, to glean the mandates and principles given by God. Preaching and teaching the full counsel will prevent false doctrine from creeping into the worship of God. The church will never err in worship if she worships according to the will of God found in the Word of God.

The Bible is the final authority and Christians must be like the Bereans so that by searching the Scriptures the church will offer worship acceptable to the Triune God, the object of Christian worship. The only acceptable worship is commanded by God and is found in the full counsel of God (Leviticus 10:1; Jeremiah 32:35).

Reading Scripture and preaching the Word of God is pleasing to God in worship (Revelation 1:3; 2 Timothy 4:2). The reading of Scripture is not sufficient; rather Scripture must be read with godly fear. The Word of God ought to be heard with a deep sense of reverence. Furthermore preaching is not enough. It must be sound preaching (Revelation 1:3; 2 Timothy 4:2; Jeremiah 26:2).

Prayer is acceptable to God in worship if it is offered through the Mediator, the Lord Jesus Christ. It is the means by which Christians express their adoration and love for the perfections of the triune God. It is the means by which they confess their sins and ask God for grace. It is the means for expressing thanksgiving and gratitude to God for His goodness and mercy (Philippians 4:6).

Baptism and the Lord's Supper were instituted by Christ. The church assembles in worship to celebrate these glorious ordinances. The sacred mystery of these divine ordinances were given for the benefit of God's covenant people when they gather to worship (Matthew 28:19; 1 Corinthians 11:23-28).

Confession of faith was normative in the apostolic church (Acts 2:42; Hebrews 4:2; Matthew 13:19). The biblical confession of faith has been replaced by testimonials. Although appropriate during times of fellowship or informal gatherings, they are not appropriate for worship.

The singing of Psalms and hymns is an expression of worship. It is offering God the words that are pleasing in His ear, if they are true. The singing of hymns during collective worship often neglects truth. The aesthetic value of singing hymns ought not to triumph over truth (Ephesians 5:19).

Gathering the tithes and offerings is part of Christian worship. However, collecting of the tithes and offerings implies that the collector is a prominent figure in liturgical worship. The picture, especially in the Old Testament, is the worshiper bringing tithes and offerings to be lifted up to God in thanksgiving (2 Chronicles 31:4-12).

The benediction is the capstone of the worship service. Throughout the worship service the Holy Spirit stimulates your senses and your mind provokes an awareness of the presence of God. The benediction symbolizes the blessing of God's hand over the life of the worshiper. What a great blessing to God's people when they understand and enjoy the prominence of true worship.

The covenant of law demands reverence to the object of worship. The third commandment is the law of reverence. "You shall not take the name of the Lord your God in vain, for the Lord will not hold him guiltless who takes His name in vain" (Exodus 20:7). It expresses the prominence of God in true worship because it calls His people to revere God's name above all other names. Due reverence for God's name is a positive comprehensive command.

Unfortunately people like to be revered and they like their name revered. The title "reverend" is not a proper title for the pastor, because it means to revere and traced to its Latin root it means "to worship". It comes from the same root word as the word venerate. For instance, this word has been grossly abused by the Roman Catholic Church in its doctrine of the veneration of saints. It literally means to worship the saints and therefore robs God of the reverence that is due to Him.

God's name reflects the sanctity of God's reputation. It is particularly important to understand the names of God. If Christians expect to understand God's nature and character, which is necessary for spiritual and true worship, they must know His names. God's supreme wisdom, infinite power, justice and truth are found in His names. The Bible gives us several names for God and each one expresses something different about God.

> Jehovah = Lord - His self existence
> El = God - His might and power

Elohim = God – Object of adoration, fear, honor and reverence
Elyon = God - Most High

Names for 2nd person of Trinity

Jesus = Joshua = savior - save from sins
Christ = Messiah = Anointed one - deliverer
Lord = Jehovah = self existence

    The third commandment asserts that the name of the Lord must not be used in vain. "You shall not take the name of the Lord in vain" (Exodus 20:7). The word "vain" comes from a Hebrew word that essentially means emptiness or worthlessness. God commanded Judah to stop bringing worthless (or vain) sacrifices to the worship service (Isaiah 1:13).
    A better understanding of the word "vain" may help understand how subtle God's name is denigrated in worship. You shall not take the name of the Lord your God in a "worthless" manner. Worth implies value and there is an eternal value in God's name.
    The Word of God is central to all Christian worship. This commandment requires God's people to receive the Word of God with boldness and sincerity and the sound preaching of the Word of God. If worship is conducted according to the Word of God, then the Scripture reading and the preaching must be in the name of the Lord. This is a serious matter revealed in the Word of God (Deuteronomy 18:15-20).
    When we promote false doctrine in worship we bring dishonor to God's name because our doctrine is built on the name of the Lord. Teaching true biblical doctrine heightens an awareness of God's prominence. It may be that some particular biblical doctrine is not particularly palatable. To teach it is to trust God with the application of His Word.
    Another way that the Lord's name is taken in vain is by deceitful worship. "Inasmuch as these people draw near with their mouths and honor Me with their lips, but have removed their

hearts far from Me, and their fear toward Me is taught by the commandment of men" (Isaiah 29:13).

If Christians neglect to call upon the name of the Lord according to Scripture, it reflects a lack of interest in God's name, therefore making God's name worthless. The Old Testament penalty for violating this commandment was death (Leviticus 24:16).

The true use of God's name in worship will bring you great joy (Psalm 5:11). The joy will come from knowing His name for the salvation of your soul.

"These things I have written to you who believe in the name of the Son of God, that you may know that you have eternal life, and that you may continue to believe in the name of the Son of God" (1 John 5:13).

When God grants you the ability to believe in the name of God you will have eternal life (1 John 5:13). Worship will become the most prominent and fulfilling joy of life.

5. A Special Place to Meet God

John 4:24

The experience and fullness of joy is in the worship of the true God. The children of God worship Him individually in their daily lives. Families worship together day by day. Then the church assembles collectively to worship. There is a special kind of joy when the saints gather to worship. For thousands of years God's congregation has assembled to find joy in worship. God's people desire to see the glory of God in worship for in it they find joy.

"The glory of the Lord filled the tabernacle" provokes the mind to wonder about the mysterious presence of God (2 Chronicles 5:14). The word "glory" has a long but variable history in the Bible. The Hebrew verb *kabed* and the noun *kabod* is most often translated into English as "glory" or "honor." The basic meaning of the word *kabod* is "heavy," "weighty," "worthiness," and "honor." It is also translated "wealth." For instance, in Genesis, Laban referred to Jacobs "wealth" (Genesis 31:1). In that context, the word "wealth" is translated from the Hebrew word *kabod*. It is necessary to inquire into this word because of the theological implications that arise from its use in the Old and New Testament. Context is the operative word in understanding the meaning of the word "glory" in the Bible.

Moses was not able to enter the tabernacle because "the cloud rested above it" (Exodus 40:34). The word "rested" comes from the Hebrew word *shaken* which means to dwell. In the context of this event in Israel, it has been referred to as the *Shekhinah glory*. The tent of meeting also called the tabernacle became the special place for the Old Testament congregation to meet God. It was at the tabernacle and later at the temple that God visited His people and they had a heightened sense of His divine presence. The glory of God is the manifestation of God's divine presence.

The proximity of God is important because the worshiper wants to engage in an intimate relationship with God. However, God's place of habitation is beyond human comprehension. Solomon understood the doctrine of God's omnipresence. "But will God indeed dwell on the earth? Behold, heaven and the heaven of heavens cannot contain You" (1 Kings 8:27). God makes His dwelling place in heaven, but He is also near His people by the power of His Spirit. Under the old covenant God used the imagery of the natural world and the passions of human life to express the reality of man in the presence of God. The Old Testament worshiper could experience the presence of God because the "glory of the Lord filled the tabernacle" (1 Kings 8:11). It was phenomenal, but very real.

The mystery of the cloud and glory in the tabernacle recorded in Exodus chapter forty may remain a mystery, but the events solidified the worship in Israel for many generations. Over four hundred years later the temple was built and dedicated in Jerusalem. Solomon, the king of Israel, along with the entire congregation assembled for the dedication of the temple. They sacrificed a great number of sheep and oxen for the event (1 Kings 8:5,63). These animals were sacrificed as burnt offerings at the entrance of the temple. The aroma of this burning animal flesh was a "sweet aroma to the Lord" (Leviticus 1:9). Consider the fact that perhaps hundreds of these animals were sacrificed over the course of the festival. Perhaps the smoke filled the temple. Have you ever been in a room filled with smoke? There is no escaping its presence. It's overwhelming. Maybe that is why the "priests could not continue ministering because of the cloud; for the glory of the Lord filled the house of the Lord" (1 Kings 8:11). It was not the bad smell of the sacrifice or the burning of the eyes that captured the attention of the priests and the people, but rather the presence of the Lord. The good experience came because they obeyed the Word of God. The special favorable presence of God is evidence of salvation and eternal life. Jesus Christ came and became a sacrifice to secure the salvation and promise of those who belong to God.

God always condescends to communicate to the feebleness of the human mind. He uses natural resources and natural experience to reveal life, so God may communicate to the rational creature. It is possible for Christians to have a feeling that does not match with the Word of God. Feelings can be very misleading. For instance, John tells Janice that he feels the Holy Spirit wants the couple to be married. Janice tells John that she feels the Holy Spirit does not want the couple to be married. Although they have two very different feelings, confusion and capricious behavior is not an attribute of the Holy Spirit. When Christians depend on feelings to establish a right relationship with God, they have to test their feelings by the Word of God which cannot err. The images, metaphors, types, and figures found in the Old Testament will help test the feelings to know if they are from God or from another source.

The eternal sanctuary is the place to offer worship to the author of life. The brevity of this secular life is forgotten in the special presence of God. It will bring joy to life when Christians offer worship that is a "sweet aroma to the Lord." The imagery from Scripture ought to illumine your mind and stimulate the senses to better understand the worth of God's divine nature. The Psalms are especially useful to remind Christians of the centrality of worship in the life of the church. The Psalms are coherent, rational, and intellectually useful to grasp the intensity the worshiper has for the object of worship. The Psalms are also touching the affections, passions, and tenderly show the love of God. The message from the Psalms is rationally pleasing and emotionally desirable.

The Psalms are full of images and word pictures that bring worship into a proper perspective. Christians may say "we have the Holy Spirit and have no need for the Old Testament language." Actually the images and word pictures found in the Old

Testament, especially the Psalms, are very useful in modern times. It is not possible to see the Holy Spirit. The power and presence of the Holy Spirit is evident in the life of the Christian believer that believes and lives according to the inspired, infallible, and inerrant Word of God. However, the worship experience will be greatly enhanced when the worshiper understands the reality of life and the nature and character of God. When God's people assemble to worship their creator, they bring with them the reality of life in this sinful world. The Psalms bring to mind the reality of human suffering. They reveal the pain, disease, and tragedy that accompany this sinful world (Psalm 69, 88). The child of God is aware of the frailties of this life, but remains confident that salvation comes from the Lord.

There was a time when David was estranged from the community of God's people; according to the Word of God David was in the wilderness of Judah. It was there that David said to God, "My soul thirsts for You; My flesh longs for You in a dry and thirsty land where there is no water" (Psalm 63:1). The language describes the whole person, both soul and body. David was "poor in spirit." He was destitute of the joy that goes with the gathering with God's people in corporate collective worship. The famished soul and the thirsty body needed to join the company of believers in the special presence of God. David concludes his lament with the memory of his previous experience in the worship service. "So I have looked for You in the sanctuary, to see Your power and glory" (Psalm 63:2). David saw reality through his memory of God's people offering worship to God in all His glory. David imagined the burnt offering and the incense, maybe so vivid that he thought he could actually feel the sensation of the aroma. He visualized the events that reveal the glory of God filling the tabernacle. The special presence of God gave David the assurance of the promise of salvation and eternal life.

Another dimension of meeting with God's people at the place God appointed was the experience of being with like minded brethren. "For I used to go with the multitude; I went with them to the house of God, with the voice of joy and praise" (Psalm 42:4). The Old Testament saints had a specific liturgy prescribed by God. If any worship took place that was not prescribed by God it was false worship. However, David remembered how they assembled to worship and everyone was in harmony because they followed God's directions. The unity among the saints was a source of joy. The praise to God was offered with one mind and one voice. The sad commentary for the 20th century church is the polarization of church doctrine especially the doctrine of corporate collective worship.

Christians live in a sinful world and like the Psalmist they experience a variety of maladies, suffering, intimidation and sometimes a sense of emptiness. They struggle against the trials and temptations that may seem to overwhelm them. Great was the suffering of the Old Testament saints. Think about being swept away in a flood and unable to find any safety. Those are the kinds of word pictures we find in the Psalms.

There are various types of Psalms that have an affective influence on the worshiper. For instance, there are Psalms of thanksgiving and adoration. "Praise is awaiting You, O God, in Zion" (Psalm 65:1). The heartbeat of worship is to praise God. Then there are Psalms of lament. There are times when Christians today cry out like the Psalmist, "Have mercy on me, O Lord, for I am weak; O Lord, heal me for my bones are troubled" (Psalm 6:2). The Royal Psalms describe God in terms of the King of the universe and the cosmic Ruler over all vassal kingdoms. All the servants of the Lord say, "Be exalted, O Lord, in Your own strength! We will sing and praise Your power" (Psalm 21:13). The Wisdom Psalms show the contrast between the wicked and the righteous in relationship to God's sovereign rule (Psalm 14 and 52). These Psalm types are found in a group of Psalms known as the "Psalms of Ascent." Many Bible scholars believe these Psalms were sung by individuals and families as they made the annual pilgrimage to Jerusalem to worship according to the

Word of God. The Psalms of Ascent help us discover the meaning of worship through the eyes of the Old Testament saints.

The Old Testament congregation sang the Psalms of Ascent as a testimony to life as it really was and the promise of God's special presence at the special place they were to meet God. The special place that God had designated was the temple in Jerusalem. The book of Psalms is replete with reminders that God has appointed a special place to meet His people. It was called His "dwelling place" (Psalm 46:4).

Psalm eighty four is another example of a zealous pilgrim describing God's special meeting place. The loveliness of the place kindles the body and soul. The Psalmist says the "heart and flesh cry out for the living God" (Psalm 84:2). There is the anticipation of the eternal Sabbath when believers will eternally offer worship to the God of the Sabbath. "For a day in Your courts is better than a thousand" (Psalm 84:10). To experience the glory of God filling the special place where God meets His people even for one minute is better than a life time of mundane existence.

To escape the afflictions, suffering, and troubles of everyday life, Christians will find comfort in the special presence of God at His special meeting place. The next fifteen chapters will examine the Psalms of Ascent. Christians today are still on a pilgrimage to Mount Zion, the heavenly city, to see the glory of the Lord.

6. God's People Desire True Worship

Psalm 120

Psalm one hundred twenty is the first of the fifteen Psalms of Ascent. They are also referred to as the Songs of degrees. These Psalms were used by God's Old Testament congregation in their preparation for religious worship at the Temple.

The Old Testament saints celebrated private and family worship throughout the year, but there were three annual feasts in which the Temple was central to worship the true and living God. As they traveled toward Jerusalem they worshipped individually and as families.

The Temple was located in Jerusalem. God designated it as the place of worship and gave the evidence by "His glory" filling the temple (1 Kings 8:11). The Temple was located nearly 100 miles to the most distant tribe. Going to worship involved a time commitment. For some of the people it was nearly one week to get to worship, a week at the temple and a week back to the village. It not only required a time commitment, it required courage to make the trip. The travel was dangerous even with the risk of the loss of life. They had to contend with the perils of nature and the threat of wild animal attacks. It was common for robbers to take advantage of traveling pilgrims. Christians ought to ponder this scenario in light of the convenience of driving a car down the street to an air conditioned building for worship.

The Psalms of Ascent is the inspired story of God's people anticipating, preparing and assembling to worship the Lord. It is a vivid description of God's people entering into the special presence of God to worship.

These Psalms are called the Psalms of Ascent because they begin with God's child far removed from the Temple. The pilgrims ascend or move up toward Mount Zion, the location of the Temple and the special dwelling place of the Lord. As they travel their anticipation of being together with God's people for worship intensifies. The normative for Christians ought to be excitement just at the thought of worship. A new reformation may occur if the Holy Spirit and the Word of God would convict Christians of the need for intensive worship. At the risk of being redundant we should remember what Karl Barth said about worship. "Christian worship is the most momentous, the most urgent, the most glorious action that can take place in human life." The Psalms of Ascent ought to arouse your passions to worship the true God according to God's Word.

The Old Testament saint described in the Psalms of Ascent is in great distress. The word "distress" is relative to agonizing fear. For instance when David numbered Israel the Lord was displeased. The Lord sent word to David that judgment may come upon Israel. David said, "I am in great distress. Please let me fall into the hand of the Lord for His mercies are very great; but do not let me fall into the hand of man" (1 Chronicles 21:13). David knew that the Lord was just, but merciful. David also understood that man is capable of inflicting trouble and misery. Likewise, in anticipation of appearing before God in worship, the Psalmist "cried to the Lord" (Psalm 120:1).

God's children cry out in distress because they live and work among the unbelievers in this world. The fervent cry from the Psalmist is a prototype for Christians in their preparation for worship.

"Woe is me, that I dwell in Meshech, that I dwell among the tents of Kedar" (Psalm 120:5)! Mesheck is in the area of Asia Minor and Kedar is East of Palestine in Arabia. It is not reasonable to believe that the Psalmist lived at both places at the same time. They were located hundreds of miles apart. The inspired Word of God refers to Mesheck and Kedar figuratively of the Old Testament saint living among fierce, barbarous, and graceless people. It was the home of mean-spirited unbelieving people.

Those unbelieving people, like unbelieving people today, are far removed from God's special presence. In fact many of them despise God. Unbelievers love to worship themselves. They hate to worship God. The church lives in a society of unbelieving people and their numbers are increasing every year. The mission of the church is to make disciples, so the converted unbelievers can join the church. Then they will discover their purpose in life is to worship God.

When God's people gather to worship there is a sense of excitement and joy. God's truth fills the soul and soothes the mind. Those who belong to God demonstrate the will to worship, because God's truth fills their souls. Their emotions are intensified as they truly and truthfully offer worship to the Lord.

The unbeliever endeavors to deceive Christians with sophistic and foolish suggestions. They tell lies with a false tongue in an attempt to drive Christians away from God. Lies and deceit are simply tools that Satan uses to divert your attention away from true Christian worship. Satan will try to convince you to worship yourself and other people, rather than the true and living God (Psalm 120:2-3).

Unbelievers will assault the church with false tongues either by tempting God's people with deceit or slandering them with lies. While Christians are busy defending themselves against the scandalous, pejorative, belittling language of the unbeliever, they are distracted from individual worship and even the anticipated worship with God's people on the Lord's Day.

Christians must devote themselves to worship the Lord. God's justice and judgment will prevail over the wicked, contemptible unbeliever. The Psalmist explains how Satan and all his followers will be punished with the "sharp arrows of the warrior" (Psalm 120:4). The warrior probably refers to the mighty hand of God as it does in Isaiah's prophecy (Isaiah 42:13). The burning coals of the broom tree is another figure of speech bringing particular attention to the wrath of God. The lies and intimidation of the unbeliever may cause distress and trouble. Be patient because God does not make empty threats. God's judgment wheel may grind slow, but it grinds exceedingly fine.

The covenant people of God not only live among an unbelieving people who hate the truth, they live among unbelieving people who hate peace (Psalm 120:6). Satan and his cadre are peace breakers and they stir up dissent, if possible even among the elect. The Lord does not snooze, but is alert and will "fight for Mount Zion" (Isaiah 31:4). The Lord will provide a special place to worship where there is peace.

Christians are able to worship God because their worship is acceptable. It is acceptable because of the peace between God and man. "Therefore having been justified by faith, we have peace with God through our Lord Jesus Christ" (Romans 5:1). Antithetically the unbeliever is treasuring up wrath in the day of wrath because unbelievers are at war with God (Romans 2:5). The unbeliever is unable to worship God, because he hates God and is at war with God. The only remedy is to have a mediator who is able to offer perfect and acceptable worship. He is the second person of the Trinity, the Lord Jesus Christ.

Although Christians live in an evil world, they can cry out to the Lord in their distress. God's people will have the desire for true worship. Individually and privately they can bow before God and worship Him in spirit and truth. Fathers ought to lead their families in worship. Pastors and church leaders have been given the responsibility to assure God's people that corporate collective worship is ordered by the Word of God. The people must hear God's truth and find peace as they assemble to worship Him. When you are surrounded by the unbelieving world with all the persecution, violence and suffering that goes along with it, cry out to the Lord. The prayer and passion in life ought to be for God to gather you along with the whole church of other like minded Christians to worship your Lord. The desire to worship is part of your preparation to worship.

Worship is not merely a present tense activity of the body. Worship is a past, present, and future tense reality involving the body and soul. Would you agree with the Psalmist? "My soul has dwelt too long with one who hates peace" (Psalm 120:6).

God's People Desire True Worship

The Psalmist remembers being with God's people for worship. He had worshipped God in unity with the congregation of God's people. It was an experience the worshiper would take back to his home and work place. He would remember, day by day, the joy of worshiping with God's truthful peaceful people.

When Christians leave the worship service, they should begin to anticipate gathering together again with God's people. They have engaged in the highest order of human responsibility. They have the privilege of being with like minded people who seek the peace of God. The only way to have peace with God is for God to grant you peace. Peace with God comes from the peace of God (Philippians 4:7).

God expects His children to live in the world He created, even when unbelievers try to deprive God's people of joy in worship. The distress may lead to pessimistic depression. The world is filled with perils like family trouble, employment dissatisfaction, ill health or a host of other troubles. The troubles of life may provoke the believer to ask the question, "Why was I born?"

Actually the question "why was I born" is a very good question. Christians will find the answer if they seek the Lord and inquire into His Word and meditate on His infallible truth.

"Where did I come from" is a question that comes to mind, even in the best of times. Every human being came from the creative power of God (Romans 1:20-21). "Why am I here" is the question that everyone must answer, sooner or later. The right answer is "to offer temporal worship to God. The wrong is "to worship myself." "Where am I going" is often the dreaded question that some people try to avoid asking. The answer depends on ones relationship with God. If one does not have peace with God, the eternal home will be a place of agonizing terror and pain. For the person who has peace with God, they will offer eternal worship to Him in a most favorable relation.

Answers to these questions are very simple yet they provoke endless discourse. More has been written on those three questions than any other in the history of mankind. They are provocative because man was created to worship God. Adam and Eve offered perfect worship to God until they began to worship the creation rather than the Creator. They "exchanged the truth of God for the lie and worshiped and served the creature rather than the creator" (Romans 1:21-25).

Much that takes place on Sunday morning is not biblical worship, but rather man-made ideas of what they think God expects in worship. The experience of peace in the worshiping congregation only comes when worshipers are unified by the Word of God.

The message of the Psalmist is "God's people desire true worship."

7. Sanctified for Worship

Psalm 121

It was a tough week at the office for John Christian. A fellow worker lied about John's performance. His wife was the target of sexual harassment at her job. Some of the school bullies picked on their son because he professed faith in Christ. Maybe these events do not happen to all Christians. Should Christians expect any less from unbelievers? Jesus said, "If they persecuted Me, they will persecute you" (John 15:20). This Psalm of Ascent describes the protection of God's children living among unbelievers.

Psalm one hundred twenty describes God's children living among the unbelievers in this world. God's child cries out in distress. The Psalmist is no different than any Christian today. He lived in a sinful world with sinful people. His lamentation is not a cry of despair. When unbelievers attack Christians at every point in life, God promises relief. Like any Christian today, the Old Testament saint had a deep yearning to be in the special presence of God with like minded brothers and sisters.

On Tuesday or Thursday or any other day, is the company of God's children in corporate collective worship vivid in your memory? Are you able to remember the songs, prayers, and the Word of God, blessing your soul. Do you remember the joy of adoring, praising and worshiping God? The Psalmist remembered and trusted God. The Psalmist was sanctified, set apart, to worship the Lord God almighty.

Christians live among unbelievers. However, Christians must be obedient to the cultural mandate (Genesis 1:28). They are like light in a dark world. The Christian mission is to engage unbelievers so that they may become disciples of Jesus Christ. The mission is noble, but taxing to the soul and body. The way to find joy, relief and refreshment is to say, "I will lift up my eyes to the hills."

There is a sense of excitement and joy as the child of God anticipates the time when he or she will join the people of God for collective worship. The memory of the previous worship service will be of great comfort while living in an unbelieving, ruthless, and cruel world. The joy and refreshment of gathering with God's people to worship the Lord has life sustaining qualities. It will remind you of your ultimate purpose when you feel helpless and standing alone in an unbelieving world.

"Where does my help come from?" The sin nature inclines Christians to seek help from earthly sources rather than looking up to Mount Zion, that celestial city from whence the divine help comes. The world is attractive because it is sensational. The world provides pseudo-satisfaction to the sensual appetite. Christians live in this world. They like this world because the sin nature naturally draws them into this world. The unbelieving world tempts Christians with its charm, its novelties, and its ways.

It is then that Christians must lift up their eyes to the hills. They must look for divine help from the all-powerful Lord of the universe. The passions of body and soul will not be satisfied unless help comes from the all sufficient God.

Psalm One hundred twenty one promises protection to God's children as they face everyday life in the unbelieving world. The protection comes while anticipating the return to worship with the believing community.

There are six promises for believers in this Psalm. God gives six promises to the pilgrim as he travels through life. The Old Testament saints probably sang this Psalm as they traveled toward Jerusalem to worship in the special presence of God.

The first promise is, "He will not allow your foot to be moved" (Psalm 121:3). The Aramaic counterpart to the word translated "moved" means one will not deviate from the right course. Life is treacherous at best. The struggle between the sin nature and the life that is dead to sin keeps Christians on the roller coaster. Christians assemble to worship God with understanding and evidence of His special presence. The greatest evidence for God's special presence is found in the grace of His living Word and His written Word. The living Word provides the sacrifice and ultimately the Mediator that makes worship acceptable to God. The written Word prescribes the acceptable offerings from the worshiper. To worship in spirit and truth is to worship the right God the right way. It brings indescribable joy to the soul.

Then Christians go back to the world of unbelief and trouble. They should carry God's promise with them because their stability is in the triune God. The true divine source helps the body and saves the soul.

During the seventeenth century a controversy arose in England primarily over purity in worship. A group of respected ministers became known as Puritans because they believed the Bible prescribed the means for pure worship, discipline, and government in the church. They eventually formed an assembly to better define uniformity of the Christian religion. They met for six years and published the *Westminster Confession of Faith and Catechisms*. They not only left the church with a biblically based explanation for worship, they left the church with an understanding of God's divine help. The confession teaches that Christians may fall into some special sin, but God's true children will never be utterly destitute of the seed of God and life of faith (*Westminster Confession of Faith*, chapter 18, section 4). To put it another way, the believer may stumble, but he or she will not fall. The occasion of public collective worship will give the believer an understanding and confidence in God's promise to keep us on the right track.

The second promise in this Psalm simply confirms the previous promise (Psalm 121:3b-4). This is one promise with dual application. It is God's promise to individuals, because it is God's promise to the church. "He who keeps you will not slumber" is God's promise to the individual Christian (Psalm

121:3b). "Behold, He who keeps Israel shall neither slumber nor sleep" is God's promise to the whole church (Psalm 121:4).

When you feel lonely and destitute in the unbelieving world, lift up your eyes heavenward and remember that the protection of God is ever present. Israel might fall asleep, but God never falls asleep. This is a promise for safe conduct as you travel through the unbelieving world toward the celestial city, Mount Zion, the place of God's special presence. It is there in God's special presence that you will find God's means of grace. The church is the place to find God's means of grace through the ministry and ordinances of God. The family is a noble institution and great comfort comes from familial relations. However, the family will not satisfy the spiritual desires of the soul. A nation may represent and protect the people, but it provides no spiritual grace. The individual believer may, in desperation, seek protection from an unreliable source. There is a way to stay on course. The church is the pillar and ground of truth (1 Timothy 3:15). Truth is always reliable. If God promises to keep his church in His hand, then certainly He will keep the individual Christian in His hand.

The third promise is, "The Lord is your keeper" (Psalm 121:5a). The third promise resonates with the gospel of John. "While I was with them in the world, I kept them in Your name. Those whom You gave me I have kept" (John 17:12). Jesus is the Shepherd and His sheep refers to the church. It is well known that sheep tend to wander off and sometimes find themselves in trouble. Jesus guarded His sheep so that none perished. Even when you travel through the valley of the shadow of death, you must remember that the Lord promised to keep you.

The fourth promise from God to the pilgrim as he travels through life is found in verses five and six (Psalm 121:5-6). The Lord is your shade at your right hand (verse 5). The sun shall not strike you by day, Nor the moon by night (verse 6). These figures of speech are very useful to describe God's generous protection for His people. The sun refers to the heat of the day and the moon refers to the cold of the night. The burning rays from an intense unbelieving world are no match for the shade that is at your right hand. The burning rays of the sun are like the miseries of human life so that they are common to all men, yet God's people have a divine shield at their right hand. The freezing nights in the wilderness are no match, because God is at your right hand.

The fifth promise is, "The Lord will preserve you from all evil; He shall preserve your soul" (Psalm 121:7). God never promises to save His children from trials and troubles, but God will protect them from the evil of their troubles. Christians must labor to understand the difference between the sin nature and the life that is dead to sin. The distinction is between the condemnation by sin and the remaining corruption of sin. It is by the grace of God that Christians struggle with sin because of the moral condition. A serious study of first eight chapters of Romans will help Christians understand this important doctrine.

The Psalmist explains the spiritual nature of His generous protection. The Lord "shall preserve your soul." The righteousness of Christ has no sin. If you have been covered with the blood of Jesus Christ your soul is eternally preserved.

> The Lord keeps the soul from the dominion of sin.
> The Lord keeps the soul from the fatal infection of error.
> The Lord keeps the soul from the puffing up of pride and lustful desire.
> The Lord keeps the soul from destruction by the world, the flesh, and the Devil.
> The Lord keeps the soul, because the soul has eternal value.

God keeps the soul in his love, for a holy kingdom unto His eternal glory. If the Lord has your soul, no harm can come to it, even in the world of unbelievers.

The sixth promise is, "The Lord shall preserve your going out and your coming in from this time forth, and even forevermore" (Psalm 121:8). Wherever God's providence carries His people in this life, He will surely guard and protect them. God brought us into this life and He will keep us when we go out of this life. Our exits and entrances are under God's promise of protection.

Like many of the Psalms, this particular Psalm is ripe with figures, types, and metaphors. It refers to eyes looking up to the hills, sleeping, slumber, heat, and cold. It is evident that these promises were understood by the Old Testament saints. What do these promises from God mean to you and to the church collectively today? By inspiration from God, His promises are given to Christians who no longer have to make that long arduous journey to worship God at the temple three times a year.

The issue is not the length of time between worship services. It's not the distance you have to travel. It's not merely the trouble of living among unbelievers. The question every Christian ought to ask in the private closet of prayer is, "does God grace me with His special presence when you gather for public collective worship? Do God's promises give you life breathing joy? Are you sanctified for worship? To put it another way, has God set you apart by His grace to worship Him?

Adoniram Judson was a missionary in Burma for forty years during the nineteenth century. He labored for years with very few converts. He was imprisoned and tortured by the natives. He suffered from failing health. He lost two wives. On his death bed Adoniram Judson said God "has not lead me so tenderly thus far to forsake me at the very gate of heaven." Lift up your eyes to the hills. Your help comes from the Lord!

8. The Church Assembles for Worship

Psalm 122

Albert Einstein said, "imagination is more important than knowledge." I'm not sure I agree with the great genius on that issue, but he does make a valid point. Imagination is a very powerful tool of the mind. Imagination is the power to formulate mental images without actually focusing on the image.

Close your eyes and remember a beautiful sight you recall from the past, perhaps standing on the North Rim of the Grand Canyon reflecting on the beauty of God's creation. The image you create in your mind's eye will produce a disturbing sensation or it will produce a feeling of peace and joy. This exposition of Psalm one hundred twenty two will be more meaningful if you have a godly imagination.

David's soul was excited when he heard the words, "Let us go into the house of the Lord." The grammar in the text reveals the nature of the author's state of mind. "Let us go" is an incomplete action that indicates the action has not yet taken place. Then in the next verse David said, "Our feet have been standing within your gates, O Jerusalem" (Psalm 122:1)! "Have been standing" is translated from a Hebrew active participle. It indicates a state of continued activity which may imply past time or present time, depending on the context.

The context, along with the grammar, describes an Old Testament Israelite, the equivalent of a New Testament church member, anticipating worship at the temple in Jerusalem. The excitement comes from the reality of a previous experience now in the imagination of the future event. We have to remember that the Old Testament congregation assembled every three or four months for worship. Imagery was extremely important to the Old Testament worshiper. It is important for the New Testament reader to put it in its proper context.

David wrote this Psalm using his memory and imagination to describe a present feeling based on past reality. It was his imagination that enabled him to take a step beyond his present experience into the reality of God's special presence in worship.

What did David see and describe in this Psalm that Christians may realize in their spiritual journey? David saw the joy in collective corporate worship. After living in the land with an unbelieving rebellious people and making a long hard journey to Jerusalem, the child of God finally steps inside the gates of Jerusalem. The Psalmist had ascended to Zion, along with the assembly of God's people to offer worship to the Lord God almighty.

Why did God's people make this long difficult journey? Was it just to attend a worship service? Perhaps they thought "some of my friends would be in church?" They always have good food and the fellowship is great. Maybe they thought "my parents always made the trip so I may as well continue the family tradition." Those may be some reasons that people "go to church today." It is not very likely that someone would risk life or limb "to go to church!"

If people would stop "going to church" and start "going to worship" there would be a reformation and revival in the land. If their purpose was to worship God, they could say as the Psalmist said, "But as for me, by Thine abundant lovingkindness I will enter Thy house. At Thy holy Temple I will bow in reverence for Thee" (Psalm 5:7). It is God's abundant love that brings His people into His presence. Love affects the special relationship that God has with His people. God's lovingkindness will stir up the soul to offer praise, honor, and glory to God. The child of God finds it a special privilege to be called to bow in reverence before the Lord God omnipotent. "To bow in reverence" refers to the humble worshiper's position before God. "For it is written: As I live, says the Lord, every knee shall bow to Me, and every tongue shall confess to God" (Romans 14:11). The bowing or bending of the knee is not necessarily the physical position in worship, although it is most appropriate. It does mean man lowers himself before God who sits high on the throne. The church must "bend the knee" to revere the dignity and majesty of the triune God.

How did the church get so far off course? It is the opinion of this writer that man-centered theology created man-centered worship. Jesus described man-centered theology in the gospel of Matthew. "And in vain they worship me, teaching as doctrines the commandments of men" (Matthew 15:9). When man decides the best doctrine for worship, it is man-centered worship. John Calvin's commentary is worth consideration.

> Since God chooses to be worshipped in no other way than according to his own appointment, he cannot endure new modes of worship to be devised. As soon as men allow themselves to wander beyond the limits of the Word of God, the more labor and anxiety they display in worshiping him, the heavier is the condemnation which they draw down upon themselves; for by such inventions religion is dishonored.

In his book *Grace and Glory*, E. L. Mascall asserts that the primary activity and function of the church is to offer praise to God. He did not say the only activity and function of the church is worship, but worship is the primary activity and function of the church. A. W. Tozer believed that Christians "are saved to worship God" (*The Purpose of Man*, by A. W. Tozer, p. 167). The purpose of the church must not be confused with the mission and ministry of the church. Although worship is the primary duty of the church, she must not ignore the mission and ministry. For some reason or the other, probably because of the sinful nature, the mission and ministry become self-centered activities rather than God- centered activities. It seems that those self-centered activities eventually lead to self-centered worship. For instance, it is so easy to pray that God will help us or heal us. It is so easy to pray for other Christians or unbelievers. However, it is difficult to pray to God, talk about God to God, and make God the subject of the prayer. A man-centered prayer primarily talks about man and a God-centered prayer talks about God. That same principle applies to worship.

When the Psalmist said, "I was glad when they said to me, Let us go into the house of the Lord" evidently he was thinking about God. He reflects on the many times he had heard the call to go and worship in the house of the Lord. This Psalm was in the mind of the pilgrim all along his long trip to Jerusalem. He imagines what it will be like to stand in Jerusalem rejoicing with all who had come to worship the Lord. Oh, what a special feeling just to anticipate corporate collective worship. How often do Christians feel the intense excitement of being with God's people to worship the Lord with the expectation of His special presence? Does the thought of true worship excite you and fill you with joy? Can you say with enthusiasm and joy to your relatives, friends and neighbors: Let us go into the house of the Lord? Let "us" gather to worship should remind Christians to worship with the voice of a cosmic choir.

The whole church must worship, thus it is "us." Old Testament Israel was a figure of the New Testament church. The Psalmist describes Jerusalem as a type for the church. He said it is compact together. The word compact comes from a Hebrew word that primarily means "joined together." A compact city is a community joined together. The true worshiping church is joined together according to the Word of God. When people meet together for worship, they must find union, concord, and common strength. If everyone has their private agenda, then the church is just like any other civic or community club.

The tribes of Israel represent all the people of God collectively. God calls His people to worship according to the "testimony" or covenant that God established for worship. Their covenant maker and object of worship is God. For that reason, they must "give thanks to the name of the Lord."

The Church Assembles for Worship

The thrones mentioned in verse five are necessary for true worship. The purpose of the thrones was to establish justice and vindicate the people of God. God's justice demands judgment and in this case it is God's justice. God has not endowed rational beings with an ultimate understanding of justice, but He has given his children a renewed mind to be used for correct thinking. The judgment seat always refers to correct thinking and correct thinking comes from a sound mind and sound words which are found in the inspired, infallible, inerrant Word of God.

Inaccurate judgments result from emotional dominance, prejudice, self-interest, and greed. Poor judgment will lead to false self-centered worship. "The judgment of God is according to truth" (Romans 2:2-3). Therefore true worship requires justice and truth. Justice and truth are necessary attributes of God, because justice and truth are necessary for the holiness of God. The triune holy God must be the object of worship. "Holy, Holy, Holy is the Lord of hosts" (Isaiah 6:3).

God's justice is ultimately expressed in and through the Lord Jesus Christ. Christ is the way for acceptable worship before the throne in heaven. Christians must understand the attribute of God called justice. If they do not understand the justice of God, they will never understand the nature and character of God and therefore we will never understand how to worship Him.

True worship awakens the whole soul to see God and God's creation. True worship awakens the mind, the emotions, and the will to see the whole counsel of God as God has revealed it in the Word of God. True worship is reverent worship because reverence to God is the highest activity of the soul. True worship steadies the mind, chastens the emotions, refreshes the imagination, reinforces the will, stirs up the desire to seek after higher things and gives men a glimpse of the character of God.

The Psalmist connects justice with peace, because the two belong together. Jerusalem is a symbol of the church and as such it symbolizes a city of peace, a city providing security and prosperity for all who love her and gather to worship the true and living God. Peace describes the condition of the true church. Peace is an emblem that the church ought to wear. Forgiveness is a necessary prerequisite for peace. If God does not forgive, there is no peace. Likewise, the siblings in the family of God must practice forgiveness to have peace in the church. When there is peace in the family there is prosperity in the family. The Psalmist places great emphasis on peace and prosperity in the congregation of God's people. He seemed compelled to make a vow. "I will now say, Peace be within you" (Psalm 122:8). The vow represents the commitment to maintain peace in the congregation.

The congregation lives among war like people. "My enemies would hound me all day, for there are many who fight against me, O Most High" (Psalm 56:2). The Psalmist also said, "I am for peace; but when I speak, they are for war" (Psalm 120:7).

When David said "Let us go into the house of the Lord" he was certain that he would find peace in the special presence of the Lord. Every Christian ought to pray for the peace of the church, because peace will insure harmony in worship.

The only peaceful remedy for peace in the church is to follow the Word of God in doctrine and practice. The Word of God may not fit your tradition, but it will bring peace.

The Psalmist made another vow that is equally important as peace. "I will seek your good" (Psalm 122:9). He must mean he will seek the best interest for the members of the congregation. "Worship is forever! It was for this that we were born again. It is to be the essence of our living, for out of worship issues everything else in life" (*Return to Worship*, by Ron Owens, p. 49). This means Christians promote the good of the church.

When you say "Let us go into the house of the Lord" will you vow for the peace and good of the church? If you do you will never forget your joy in worship!

9. The Mercy of God in Worship

Psalm 123

What do you talk about on the way to worship on the Lord's Day? Is it causal conversation about the mundane affairs of life? Maybe someone says "I hope the preacher finishes on time today." In the comfort of the car there is probably some discussion about something.

Now let's shift to a different scenario. It is 800 B.C. and the Old Testament families are walking to Jerusalem to worship. For the most distant tribes, it would take days of rigorous risky travel. They had plenty of time to talk to each other. What did they talk about?

"I cried to the Lord" (Psalm 120:1). "My help comes from the Lord" (Psalm 121:2). "Let us go into the house of the Lord" (Psalm 122:1). "Unto You I lift up my eyes" (Psalm 123:1). The "Lord" seems to be the primary subject as the Old Testament families travelled to Jerusalem.

Puritan congregations, like the Old Testament congregation, talked about the Lord. The Puritan minister would exhort the congregation in this manner. "The whole day is to be celebrated as holy to the Lord, both in public and private, as being the Christian Sabbath. To which end, it is requisite, that there be a holy cessation or resting all that day from all unnecessary labors; and an abstaining, not only from all sports and pastimes, but also from all worldly words and thoughts." The Puritan congregation like the Old Testament congregation engaged in words and thoughts about God, especially on the day of public worship.

The contemporary church has lost a sense of the divine presence to accommodate the cultural craving for self-fulfillment. There are no short cuts. The only way to talk about God is to use the words that describe God. In his book, *The Essence of*

Christian Doctrine, Martin Murphy gives a brief description of God. It is only a brief summary, but it is a starting point.

> Our heavenly Father is sovereign, dignified above all other personalities, and demonstrates the most excellent divine perfections that can be imagined (Isaiah 6:1-3).
> Our heavenly Father is the perfect Father (Matthew 5:48). Our heavenly Father is the most wise Father (1 Timothy 1:17).
>
> Our heavenly Father is the most loving Father (1 John. 4:16).
>
> Our heavenly Father has unsearchable riches (Colossians 1:16).
>
> Our heavenly Father truly understands and applies the doctrine of forgiveness. If the guilt of sin is not forgiven and the particular sins are not forgiven, you will forever be tormented in your soul (Ephesians 4:32).
>
> Our heavenly Father is the best Father, because He can reform His children (Acts 16:14).
>
> Our heavenly Father will polish His children and make them shining vessels to His glory (Isaiah 60:1).
>
> Our heavenly Father is the oldest Father in the Universe (Daniel 7:9).
>
> Our heavenly Father lives forever (Isaiah 57:15).

The Old Testament saints also talked about the misery of living among unbelievers. The child of God begins his journey to Jerusalem thus leaving the land of Mescheh and Kedar. The worshiper describes the troublesome surroundings and how he cries out to God for help. The Psalmist lifts us his eyes to the hills and finds his confidence in the Lord. The worshiper imagines what it will be like to be in the special presence of God and among fellow believers.

Psalm one hundred twenty three continues to contrast the holiness of God and sinfulness of this world. To find relief from the sinfulness of this world, find the holiness of God. "Exalt the Lord our God, and worship at His holy hill; For the Lord our God is holy" (Psalm 99:9). The first order in worship is to lift up the eyes to the Lord. Preparation for worship ought to include discussion about God. His nature, character, and attributes ought to capture the attention of Christians. Then when they gather to worship it is fitting and proper to say: "Unto You I lift up my eyes, O YOU who dwell in the heavens" (Psalm 123:1).

The subject and object of worship is God. Congregations often get excited during worship and have emotional responses that God has not commanded in worship (Leviticus 10:1). There are two dangers in public worship. The first danger is a strict liturgy that does not allow for spontaneity of the soul to have an emotional response to God. Just as bad is when the emotions overrule the necessity of knowing God and what God desires in worship. The best way to begin worship is to lift up your eyes to the Lord God of heaven and earth. When you lift up your eyes what do you see? Do you see God?

> Look and you will find God.
> Look and you find Him in His creation.
> Look and you find Him in Holy Scripture.
> Look and you find Him in the Lord Jesus Christ.
> Look and you find Him in the Word of God.
> Look and you find Him in the sacraments.
> Look and you find Him in prayer.
> Look and you will find Him in the worship God has commanded .

The Psalmist seems to have command of his eyes. He calls them "my eyes." It would be negligent to not use the eyes that God has given him. Within the context of worship the eyes focus on the object of worship; "O You, who dwell in the heavens." The shift from this world to the spiritual world, the unseen world, may escalate a sense of insecurity. Human beings, even Christians, may experience an insecure feeling, because they are dependent on God who is Spirit.

Christians have to understand something of the spirituality of God. He is immaterial without body or bodily parts. Experience with the material world does not relate directly with the spiritual dimension. However, anyone can deduce from material things that there must be a spiritual dimension. When they are enabled by the power of the Holy Spirit to believe, then God reveals that spiritual dimension in the Word of God.

The worshiping soul lifts up his eyes to the One who dwells in the heavens. God always provides the means for the worshiper to know the object of worship. The eyes as a figure of speech represent the means by which the worshiper may understand who to worship and how to worship.

There are two domestic metaphors in Psalm one hundred twenty three that are very useful. They explain how Christians ought to focus upon God and pay attention to God's every command in worship.

The *New American Standard Bible* describes the relation of the servant to the master. "Behold, as the eyes of the servants look to the hand of their master" (Psalm 123:2). It is proper that there are many servants, but one master. This metaphor describes how the servant's eyes look to the hands of the master. The master of the house in Eastern cultures has long used his hands to communicate to household servants. A snap of the finger or a wave of the hand instructs the servant of the master's desire. The servant knows very well the desire of his master. The women also trained their household servants to pay attention to every visible command.

These metaphors manifestly describe the worshiper and the object of worship. The simple doctrine is that God is the center of the theater. All eyes are upon Him. The essence of life, being, and consciousness will connect with the triune God giving glory to the Father, through the work of the Son, by the power of the Holy Spirit.

If worship is not affecting the worshiper, then the spiritual eyes are blind or they need washing out. There are two reasons people cannot see God in worship.

Jesus describes spiritual blindness in the gospel of John. In a conversation with the Jews, Jesus explained that if they were His disciples they would remain in His word and they would know the truth. Finally Jesus asked them a rhetorical question. "Why do you not understand my speech? Because you are not able to listen to My word. You are of your father the devil, and the desires of your father you want to do" (John 8:43-44). Paul explains the same concept in his letter to the Ephesians. Paul explains how unbelievers "having their understanding darkened, being alienated from the life of God, because of the ignorance that is in them, because of the blindness of their heart" (Ephesians 4:18). If this condition exists, pray for the grace of God that the spiritual blindness may be healed by the work of the Holy Spirit. The Lord Jesus came to "save His people from their sins" (Matthew 1:21), so they might see again.

Another reason that people cannot see God in worship is ignorance. The biblical text is quite clear about the ignorance of God in the life of a professing believer.

> For though by this time you ought to be teachers, you need someone to teach you again the first principles of the oracles of God; and you have come to need milk and not solid food. For everyone who partakes only of milk is unskilled in the word of righteousness, for he is a babe. But solid food belongs to those who are of full age, that is, those who by reason of use have their senses exercised

to discern both good and evil (Hebrews 5:12-14; also see 1 Corinthians 3:2;).

This text applies to all professing believers as they progress in their knowledge of the divine nature of God and the metaphysical character of God's children. However, the text is especially useful for Christians engaged in public worship. As God's children grow in their understanding of the triune God, they should say, as the Psalmist did, "So our eyes look to the Lord our God, Until He has mercy on us" (Psalm 123:2).

They look to the Lord with eyes of hope, anticipation, and expectation until the Lord has mercy on them. The metaphor of the household servants ought to be understood in light of the Apostles' understanding of being a slave of Jesus Christ (2 Timothy 2:24; Titus 1:1; James 1:1; 2 Peter 1:1). In biblical terms a slave, a servant if it is more palatable to your vocabulary, lives and exists to serve their master. They look at his every command, since they are totally dependent on the master for everything in life. The good servant serves the master and the good master shows mercy to the servant. Likewise, God's worshipers desire mercy and God is merciful.

The words from the lips of a godly man are "have mercy on us, O Lord, have mercy on us" (Psalm 123:3). The godly man calls out to the Lord with an emphatic entreaty. It is a command of entreaty expressing an urgent request to the Master. You would have to ask the question: "why is this child of God so disturbed?" Why is he so upset? Why is he crying out for mercy?

The answer is in the text. "Have mercy on us, O LORD, have mercy on us! For we are exceedingly filled with contempt. Our soul is exceedingly filled with the scorn of those who are at ease, with the contempt of the proud" (Psalm 123:3-4).

The child of God was overwhelmed with derision and scoffing of those who were self-confident. His unbelieving neighbor boasted in a false security of worldly assets. The unbeliever finds security in some secular title or secular wealth and flaunts it to the humble believer. They love to mock Christians! The child of God is overwhelmed with the contempt of the proud. John Calvin comments, "that rich and proud men treat the church with insolent triumph; for it commonly happens that those who are elevated in the world, look down with contempt upon the people of God" (*Calvin's Commentaries*, vol. 2, Psalm 123). The wickedness of prosperity is an instrument used to afflict God's people. The Psalmist simply expresses the reality of life in this world. The haughtiness of pride and arrogance afflicts you so that your soul is exceedingly filled with pain and sorrow.

  Is there any solution to all this? Yes! Cry out like the Psalmist, "Have mercy on us O Lord Have mercy on us." The remedy for contempt and scorn is the Lord's mercy. The burden of sin and misery may trouble your soul, but you will find relief if you look to the Lord your God for mercy.

10. The Guardian of the Church

Psalm 124

This Psalm was composed for God's people after a threatening or dangerous encounter with the enemy. It is a Psalm of thanksgiving for God's generous protection. Christians need a guardian for body and soul. The words of Jesus resonate with this doctrine. "If the world hates you, you know that it hated Me before it hated you" (John 15:18). Hatred leads to persecution. Jesus also said, "If they persecuted Me, they will also persecute you" (John 15:20).

The people of God live among the unbelievers of this world. These unbelieving people are far removed from God's special presence and many of them despise God. Unbelievers love to worship themselves. They hate to worship God. Christians live in a society of unbelieving people. The United States is a nation of syncretistic religious organizations. Relative to worship, the word "syncretized" refers to mixing two religious principles into one. Syncretism is "the union of two or more opposite beliefs, so that the syncretized form is a new thing. It is not always a total fusion, but may be a combination of separate segments that remain identifiable compartments" (*Evangelical Dictionary of Theology*, ed. Walter A. Elwell, p. 1062). Syncretized worship has made the Christian church one of the most discombobulated among all the religious organizations. The Bible has become the book of choice, as long as it may be interpreted with a variety of meanings. The apocalypse of entertainment in worship is quickly eroding the once strong evangelical church. However, God's true church will always offer thanksgiving for the privilege of public worship.

Psalm one hundred four is the response of God's redeemed people as they lift up their voices in adoration, praise and thanksgiving. The Old Testament congregation expressed their love and adoration to God. God saves His people so they will be able to worship Him. Jesus Christ redeemed His people with a cosmic show of power over death and damnation. Christ delivered His church from the hands of the enemy. The church will always be delivered from the hands of deceitful unfaithful men in due time, because the church has a Guardian to protect it from ruin and destruction. Worship is the only expression of religion that connects God's people with the past, present, and future church.

The response from the individual worshiper is, "If it had not been the Lord who was on our side" the people of God would have perished at the hand of their enemy. Likewise, the church ought to acknowledge God's generous protection. God's redeemed people ought to lift up their voices in adoration, praise, and thanksgiving.

Psalm one hundred twenty four has language that may appear ambiguous. Notice the language in verses three through seven.

> Men would have swallowed us alive (Psalm 124:3).
> Water overwhelm us (Psalm 124:4).
> Flood swept over our soul (Psalm 124:5).
> Prey to their teeth (Psalm 124:6).
> Soul escaped the fowler (Psalm 124:7).

These are figures of speech and they have a distinctive message. To interpret these figures of speech without taking away God's intended meaning is the goal. The text identifies David as the author of this Psalm. Some critical scholars believe this Psalm was written at or around the time of the Babylonian invasion and captivity of Israel in 586 B.C. The Hebrew text indicates David is the author. The historical circumstances of David's life around 1000 B.C. could validate his authorship. This Psalm describes a calamitous event suffered by the author and the entire community of God's people. David's life was filled with affliction and torment by his enemies and even his own family. There is no reason to question David's authorship of this Psalm around 1000 B. C.

God's people have always been ridiculed and despised by the devil and all his minions. Ungodly people are hostile towards the people of God. The Egyptians subjugated the Israelites. The Philistines tried to kill the Israelites. David's children and some of his faithful followers turned against David. The Psalm also describes the invasion of Israel by the Assyrians and the Babylonian invasion. During the life and ministry of Christ the Pharisees opposed the true church. In 8th century A.D. the Islamic forces tried to overthrow Europe, and thus destroy Christianity. This Psalm applies to the entire history of God's people. Today the church still has enemies. The application of the metaphors in this text requires serious study. They must not be taken out of context, but considered in the light of the whole counsel of God.

The dominance of cultural elites in the western world has brought great distress to the church. Management theories in the market place ought to consider the ethical dimension and equity for all parties. Instead they get as much as they can and give as little as they can. Managerial concepts used in the public sector have invaded the church. The sacrifice of biblical worship was necessary to accommodate and manage large groups of diverse people. Unbiblical therapeutic counseling replaced the biblical ministry of the church. Entertainment regularly replaces biblical commandments to worship God. The application of this Psalm is as contemporary as today's newspaper.

These figures of speech are defined in two similar categories. A metaphor treats one thing as if it was something else. A simile describes something in terms of being like something else. The metaphor of the water is pregnant with visual lessons. The water metaphor is appropriate to get the attention of people living in an arid climate and treacherous terrain. The writer begins with water, then moves on to a stream, and finally becomes swollen waters. From the lesser to the greater represents the exponential force by which the enemy intends to destroy the church. The ungodly people are described in terms of a flood that would sweep away the soul with its fury and power. Then a simile in verse seven paints the picture of the soul escaping like a bird escapes from a snare.

Obviously the ungodly people are described as wild animals that would have swallowed God's children alive. Even clearer in verse six we see that Christians are prey to their teeth. We know what animals do with their prey; they tear it apart and devour it. Christians face total mutilation. The forces of evil will not skimp when they attempt to destroy Christians. The forces of evil will attack body and soul.

The Christian mind is the primary target of the godless unbeliever. God commands His children to, "be like-minded toward one another, according to Jesus Christ" (Romans 15:5). Then the old serpent will say, "Did God really mean for you to be like-minded with other Christians?" Satan will work on the mind with his mouth. He will charm you and try to convince you that you have your own mind and can think for yourself.

The Devil is a crafty fellow. His whole purpose in time and space is to deceive as many people as possible. Christians may say, "I'm not afraid of the Devil" but that is not really the issue. The more important question; is the Devil afraid of Christians?

Some people, even professing Christians, seem to be very agreeable to the Devil's scheme. There is the story of a lady who never spoke ill of anybody. A friend told her that she probably says good things about the Devil. The lady responded by explaining that we do have to admire the Devil's persistence.

The Devil is not only persistent, he is a cunning creature. The snake has often been seen as the prototype of the Devil. A snake is quiet and sometimes charming, just like the Devil. However, his charm is as poisonous as a rattlesnake. The Devil is not only a creepy, sneaky, dangerous character, the Devil is deadly. Peter's inspired words render a graphic picture from the animal world. "Your adversary the devil walks about like a roaring lion, seeking whom he may devour" (1 Peter 5:8).

The work of the Devil is extensive. The Devil will use philosophy, science, politics, education, and religion to promote his cause. He will resort to anything that will cause a professing believer to offer worship to false gods. His goal is to prevent Christians from offering true worship to the true God. Satan tries to deceive individual Christians. Although the devil works to deceive one Christian at a time, his goal is to persuade the whole church to worship him. Does that mean that the church can be destroyed? Jesus said even the most evil forces on earth cannot prevail against the church.

The wickedness in this world may violently beset itself against God's people. God's people may feel defenseless, but they must never forget that the Lord is on their side. Godly people may appear to be powerless against the power of the world, but they must not fall into despair. Isaiah declares that "God is with us" (Isaiah 8:10). "The Lord is on our side." Godly people trust and wait upon the Lord.

The goodness of God is the balm that calms the soul. In response to the goodness of God, the people of God say in unison, "Blessed be the Lord" (Psalm 124:6). The word "bless" or "blessing" is often used impulsively without any mitigating thought. Ancient Middle Eastern Cultures used the blessing to endow someone with some beneficent intent. The words associated with the blessing had to be accompanied with a physical response to confirm the endowment, normally the laying on the hands (Genesis 48:13-14). Since there is no physical contact by God, His blessing must be associated with His favorable presence in goodness and peace. When the subject, a child of God, blesses the object, the Lord God, it is an expression of adoration and praise.

Satan sets his trap, but Christians can say as the Psalmist did "Our soul has escaped as a bird" from the snare of the trapper.

There was a time when your soul was in bondage to the evil one. You were surrounded by unbelief, selfishness, and worldliness. God gave you the power to escape. You were in bondage to false worship, but God gave you freedom to worship the true and living God.

Then what do you say to God? "Our help is in the name of the Lord, Who made heaven and earth." Everybody said, "Blessed be the Lord."

The profundity of verse eight and the inferences that might be drawn from it exceed the purpose of this book. Those few words call attention to the condition of the human race. However, in the context the specific audience is God's people. The Creator, Sustainer, and Provider is, "our help." Man is helpless from beginning to end. Man cannot save himself and he cannot raise himself from the dead. "Our help" almost sounds superficial, but the Word of God is never superficial.

In this Psalm God's people suffer as a result of wicked men who hate God, but they are unable to cause God any suffering, so they prey upon God's people. Christ redeemed His people with a cosmic show of power over death and damnation. Christians must, with more vigor and passion, expect the church to be delivered from the hands of the enemy.

When things are in great disorder your help is in the name of the Lord. When Christians feel the pressure from ungodly criticism, they must remember that the Lord is on their side. When Satan appears to be in control remember that the church has the Lord God almighty to protect it from ruin and destruction, so the church may gather and worship in spirit and truth. If the church has a Guardian, you as an individual have a Guardian.

God protects and saves His church so the church can worship Him. God liberates His children from Satan's bondage and gives them freedom to worship the true and living God. The inspired infallible story of Jesus healing the blind man recorded in the gospel of John reveals the difference in bondage to Satan and freedom to worship God (John 9:1-38). The Pharisees were unbelievers and they despised the Lord of the Sabbath. The man born blind believed the Lord and "worshipped Him" (John 10:38).

Is the Lord on your side? Has He protected you with His righteous right hand? Is your help in the name of the Lord? If the answer is yes, yes, yes, then blessed be the name of the Lord. Has the Lord God given you new sight by grace through faith in the Lord Jesus Christ by the power of the Holy Spirit? If the answer is yes, worship Him!

As Christians go to sleep at the end of each Lord's Day, they ought to give the Lord much thanks for the precious gift of the local gathering of His saints. There is profit in every way, today, in the fellowship of the saints, the united prayer of the church, the preaching of the Word, the partaking of the Lord's Supper, and the singing of spiritual songs. What a privilege it is to go up to the heavenly Jerusalem and worship our triune God!

11. Security for the Redeemed Worshiper

Psalm 125

Some of the most profound ideas known to man can be found in the Book of Proverbs and the Book of Psalms. "He who heeds the word wisely will find good, And whoever trusts in the Lord, happy is he" (Proverbs 16:20). Another translation uses "blessed" instead of "happy." "Blessed is he who trusts in the Lord" (Proverbs 16:20, *New American Standard Bible*).

The word "happy" in the *New King James Bible* and the word "blessed" in *New American Standard Bible* is translated from the Hebrew word *esher*. It was later translated from the Septuagint Greek text into English as "blessed."

The words blessed and happy are used often in the Word of God. What is blessedness or happiness? The way Americans generally use the word happy has more to do with sinful pleasures rather than peace and contentment.

The word happy comes from an old English word "hap." The word "hap" originally referred to "luck" or "good fortune." After the French Revolution and the rise of rationalism in the 18th century, the word happy became associated with the war cry of the French Revolution. "Liberty, fraternity, and equality" became a synonym for happiness to the mind of the impoverished Frenchman. It was the kind of happiness that would permeate the entire western world.

People look for happiness in every imaginable place. The study of philosophy will not bring happiness. Philosophy is a friend of wisdom and will be a blessing to those who study it. Education will not bring happiness. True education is a discipline that teaches one how to think. A true education may provide the tools to understand the blessing of knowing God. Worldly pleasure may appear to bring happiness. However, worldly pleasure only stimulates the sensations that allegedly produce pleasure. Material wealth may provide the sensual pleasure, but wealth will not buy happiness. People through the ages in every part of the world seek happiness through religious activity.

The Bible describes a different kind of happiness that in ancient times was known as "a blessing." He who trusts in the Lord will not find the kind of happiness the people seek in philosophy, education, pleasure, wealth, or religion. The joy of the blessed man is God's special grace. The blessing is most evident when the child of God offers biblical worship to God.

Worship begins by trusting God without equivocation. "Blessed are all those who put their trust in Him" (Psalm 2:12). "Oh taste and see that the Lord is good; Blessed is the man who trusts in Him" (Psalm 34:8).

God's blessing has nothing to do with luck, charm, or good fortunes. God's blessing is a condition that brings His children security in an insecure world. New Testament saved sinners are just like those Old Testament saints described in these Psalms of Ascent. They live in a hostile world filled with anger, hatred, and contempt. The modern psychological terminology might be stated in terms of living in an insecure world.

Insecurity in this world comes from doubt, uncertainty, and fear. The sinful nature is the cause of these destructive conditions. These internal conditions are often confronted by outward threats from the people we live around. What Christians need is to find refuge and security from those who hate peace and seek to destroy them. Christians will find refuge and security by trusting in the Lord. Trust may be understood from two perspectives.

Temporal trust in the material substance of this world is self imposed. It may be philosophy, education, material wealth, worldly pleasures or religion. It will always be temporary if it is self created. Nebuchadnezzar expressed temporal trust in the ultimate sense. The prophet Isaiah speaking for God about Nebuchadnezzar said, "For you have trusted (feel secure) in your wickedness; you have said, 'No one sees me'; Your wisdom and your knowledge have warped you; And you have said in your heart I am and there is no one else besides me" (Isaiah 47:10). There is a sense in which temporal security is false trust. The psychologist might use the word insecurity to describe false trust, but in the end "I am" will have to give account.

The evangelical church applies the "insecurity syndrome" to worship. Pastors and church leaders try to make people comfortable in worship. It has been said more than once that "we're trying to be sensitive to all worship styles so the younger generation can be in touch with their emotions." The desire to please everyone with worship styles "which He (God) had not commanded" disregards the holiness of God (Leviticus 10:1).

Ultimately the insecurity will increase because there is no objective standard. Christians need a wake up call to be reminded that God did not ordain worship to make people feel happy. True worship is not about meeting personal needs. God ordained worship so that His people might find security in their worship to the Creator, Sustainer, and Governor of the universe.

Eternal trust is the essential dependence in the Lord (Psalm 125:1). When Christians trust in the Lord it is like Mount Zion which cannot be moved, but abides forever. The Psalmist uses a mountain as a metaphor for splendor, majesty, and strength. Mount Zion, the location of Jerusalem and the temple of God in the Old Testament, is 2550 feet above sea level. The mountains that surrounded Jerusalem protected the city from its enemies. When the Old Testament congregation came to Jerusalem to worship they, figuratively speaking, escaped from the enemy. So the mountain is a fit analogy for how the Lord protects his people by His strength and power. The believer is saved, not by his or her own strength, but by the power of the Lord. The mountain is also an emblem of stability and security. The mountain of the Lord can never be moved and our trust in Him will last from this time forth and forever. The Lord protects His church from destruction. Even though the Lord wraps His mighty eternal arms around you, trials, tribulations and temptations will still come your way. Understanding the biblical doctrine of perseverance will bring comfort when the enemy assaults you. The Psalmist said even though "The cords of the wicked have bound me" (Psalm 119:61), "I trust in the Lord" (Psalm 31:6). The ungodly will persecute you and you may be tempted to turn aside from the way of righteousness, but remember that God's grace is for God's people. If you belong to God because of the sacrifice of Jesus Christ on your behalf and powerfully applied by the Holy Spirit, you will preserve to the end.

The child of God has received God's grace, but may be tempted to sin. The Psalmist warns God's people to be careful "lest the righteous reach out their hands to iniquity" (Psalm 125:3). Temptations will visit believers from time to time and very often from external sources. Wicked men will try anything and go to any length to get God's children to turn away from righteousness. However, "No temptation has overtaken you except such as is common to man; but God is faithful who will not allow you to be tempted beyond what you are able, but with the temptation will also make the way of escape" (1 Corinthians 10:13). No temptation or trial will remove the true believer from the hand of God. Sin belongs to man, not to God. "Let no one say when he is tempted, 'I am tempted by God' for God cannot be tempted by evil, nor does He Himself tempt anyone. But each one is tempted when he drawn away by his own desires and enticed" (James 1:13-14).

"Do good, O Lord, to those who are good, and to those who are upright in their hearts" (Psalm 125:4). The "upright in heart" refers to justification by faith. Justification by faith is the foundation for a right relationship with God. The Word of God has a complete expression of the upright in heart. "Moreover whom He predestined, these He also called; whom He called, these He also justified; and whom He justified, these He also glorified" (Romans 8:30). The only security in this world for Christians is to know that their security comes from another world.

In the absence of a glimpse into the next world the Lord gives us an example of what it is like to be secure in His everlasting arms. "Those who trust in the Lord are like Mt. Zion" (Psalm 125:1). Some people are like sand, ever shifting and sinking. Some people are like the sea; they are restless and unsettled. Some people are like the wind; they are uncertain and inconsistent. But those who trust in the Lord are like a mountain; they are strong, stable, and secure.

The Psalmist also warns those who come to worship that there is such a thing as false security. "As for such as turn aside to their crooked ways, the Lord shall lead them away with the workers of iniquity" (Psalm 125:5).

The phrase "turn aside to their crooked ways" could literally be translated "to the way of perversion." This text must refer to hypocrites. This text does not refer to Christians who are tempted and fall into some sin, maybe a grievous sin. It does refer to those who are not justified by faith.

> Hypocrites! Well did Isaiah prophesy about you, saying:
> These people draw near to Me with their mouth,
> And honor Me with their lips,
> But their heart is far from Me,
> And in vain they worship Me,
> Teaching as doctrines the commandments of men.
> (Matthew 15:7-9)

Hypocrisy in worship is the result of a counterfeit profession of faith. Jesus simply ratifies the Old Testament teaching that man-made worship is worship that the Lord had not commanded. Hypocrites are the authors of man-made worship.

This Psalm must be understood in its proper context. The people of God are making a long journey to Mount Zion to worship the Lord. They probably sang this Psalm along the way, thinking about the mountains and how that is analogous to the trust they had in the Lord. Then the Psalm shifts and lays out a warning for the worshiping pilgrims. How can worshipers who trust the Lord turn aside to their own crooked ways?

You can see the sense of anxiety expressed in this pilgrim song. The pastor of God's flock ought to be especially anxious. His distress is that all in Israel are not true Israelites. Instead of resisting temptation in the evil day, the professing Christian will put forth his hand into iniquity. In the words of the Psalmist they will follow the rod of the wicked. They will turn aside unto their crooked ways. They will follow their own philosophy. They will follow their own material wealth. They will follow their own worldly pleasures. They will follow their own religious beliefs. They will teach "as doctrines the commandments of men."

Every Christian should ask the question: Am I a true Israelite or professing Israelite? Am I a true Christian and truly trusting the Lord or do I just profess the Christian religion? According to the Word of God Christians may have an infallible assurance of faith. Jesus came to, "save his people from their sins" (Matt 1:21) and, "to give his life as a ransom for many" (Matt.20:28). "Furthermore God said, "I give them eternal life, and they shall never perish, and no one shall snatch them out of my hand" (John 10:28). One of the grounds of our assurance is the infallible truths and promises of salvation. Another ground of infallible assurance is the inward evidence of those graces unto which these promises are made. The inward evidence includes every aspect of sanctification and the spiritual maturity of the believer. The third ground of assurance is the testimony of the Spirit of adoption witnessing with our spirit that we are the children of God. Again God speaks clearly that "he who believes in the Son of God has the witness in himself" (1 John 5:10). Finally the ground of assurance is work of the Holy Spirit sealed unto the day of redemption. It must be remembered that feelings and emotions are not the grounds of assurance.

The final words in our Psalm explain how Christians can know they have an infallible assurance of faith. "Peace be upon Israel." Peace is the mark of true Christian trust. Peace means there is a right relationship with God and with God's people. Peace is the mark of one who trusts in the Lord. Peace is the mark of the upright in heart. Peace is the sign of salvation that comes from above.

God's peace provides security in an insecure world. If we put this Psalm in the context of the Old Testament worshiper, we find that worship is central to life and the experiences of life. Christian worship is central to the entire experience of this life and the reality of the life to come.

God's benediction to those who trust in Him: Peace be upon Israel.

12. Preparation for Heavenly Worship

Psalm 126

The mention of the word worship may bring to mind one of several styles found when the local church assembles on Sunday morning. It may bring to mind a strict liturgy. One or perhaps several persons are center stage and the audience observes and maybe even sings a hymn. Another scenario may be that of a performer in the theater and the audience observing and listening to every word. Anyhow, the word worship creates different pictures in the mind of different people.

There is a sense in which polarity is normal with the use of words. For instance, love and hate stand in a stark dichotomous relationship. There are degrees of love and hate, but always a point of demarcation. The fundamental concept of love and hate as an emotional response depends on the disposition of the human will. There is either a desire to love or hate. People are inclined to love or hate. This fundamental principle may be applied to worship. They either love or hate worship. Likewise people experience sadness and joy. These concepts ultimately affect our whole being, body and soul.

During the course of the day we meet a variety of contingencies that bring either sadness or joy. For example, if you wake up in the morning with a virus infection it probably produces pain which provokes sadness. However if you wake up to the good news that you have inherited a large sum of money, there is a sense of joy. The principle is universal. It violates the law of non-contradiction to say that you experience sadness and joy at the same time in the same relationship.

The application of this principle in the Christian life is profound. God's revelation will produce sadness or joy. God's revelation simply means that God makes Himself known. The application of this principle is universal, "because what may be known of God is manifest in them, for God has shown it to them. For since the creation of the world His invisible attributes are clearly seen, being understood by the things that are made, even His eternal power and Godhead, so that they are without excuse" (Romans 1:19-20). It is not possible for anyone to escape the knowledge of God. God reveals Himself to the whole human race. God's revelation of His power and authority descends so that its effect is profoundly powerful. For some people God's revelation brings sadness. For others, God's revelation not only brings joy, but it is pure joy.

Why is that so? Some people are blind with unbelief so that God's revelation reminds them of God's power and authority over them. Since they want to be in control, they try to avoid any relationship with God. Furthermore, they know that God's power and authority is eternal. They understand their sad condition. Since they have no peace, they engage in war against God's people who do have peace.

Those who have been born again by the power of the Holy Spirit are awake to the truth and the light of eternal salvation so that God's revelation is joy. God's revelation of Himself is particularly joyful when the people of God gather to worship.

Psalm 126 is called the joyful return to Zion in the *Geneva Study Bible*, and so it is, but only because God made Himself known to His people. This Psalm is appropriately placed in this order of the Psalms of ascent, because it is a step up toward Mount Zion, the Temple of God, which was the place of worship. This Psalm reminded the Child of God to prepare for worship. Preparation for heavenly worship is a time of great joy for the believer. Believers are captive to their Father and they desire to prepare to meet Him. Keep in mind that unbelievers are captive to their father, the Devil (John 8:42-44).

This Psalm brings the concept of captivity into the realm of worship. "When the Lord brought back the captivity of Zion" the text describes great deliverance from oppression. Bible scholars have long debated the source of oppression which would possibly determine the date of the Psalm. Many good godly men argue that it was deliverance from the Babylonian captivity. However, it is not impossible for it to have been David's Psalm after the skirmish with his son Absolom when David had to leave Jerusalem. Arguments over the specific deliverance detract from the more important doctrines of this Psalm.

Whatever the captivity was, it was great because it was the Lord who accomplished the release. Just stop and think about the times you have experienced the feeling of being held captive. Maybe it was a habit that captivated you. Maybe you got in financial debt and felt you were captive to the debtor. Have you ever come to the place that it seemed as if you had come to the end of the road? There was no place to turn except to turn to the gracious hand of the Lord for release from the captivity of that time. The principle of "being held captive" applies to the soul and eternity, just like it does for the mundane things of this life. Jesus explained this principle and it is worth repeating. Believers are captive to their Father and unbelievers are captive to their father.

When God changes the heart of a sinner thus enabling him or her to believe, it is the greatest release from captivity of all time and eternity. Formally bound to evil without hope of eternal life, God releases the sinner from hopelessness and eternal damnation, to life with Christ forever. The soul is recreated to worship the heavenly father in spirit and truth. God explained this doctrine and was recorded by the inspired Apostle Paul.

> And you He made alive, who were dead in trespasses and sins, in which you once walked according to the course of this world, according to the prince of the power of the air, the spirit who now works in the sons of disobedience, among whom also we all once conducted ourselves in the lusts of our flesh, fulfilling the desires of the flesh and of the mind, and were by nature children of wrath, just as the others. But God, who is rich in mercy, because of His

great love with which He loved us, even when we were dead in trespasses, made us alive together with Christ (by grace you have been saved), and raised us up together, and made us sit together in the heavenly places in Christ Jesus, that in the ages to come He might show the exceeding riches of His grace in His kindness toward us in Christ Jesus. For by grace you have been saved through faith, and that not of yourselves; it is the gift of God, not of works, lest anyone should boast. For we are His workmanship, created in Christ Jesus for good works, which God prepared beforehand that we should walk in them. (Ephesians 2:1-10)

Worship begins and ends with the glory of God. The questions that follow will put the Ephesian text in perspective.

1. Do you understand the love of God in light of your sinfulness? Have you experienced the glory of God's love in your new birth?

2. Have you been raised up together with Christ?

3. Are you resting in Christ, so that your life is one great huge worship experience?

If you cannot answer yes to those questions, then perhaps you need to remember that you may be "dead in trespasses and sins." Then pray for God to have mercy on your soul. If you can answer yes to those questions, then you may continue to see the "exceeding riches of God's grace in His kindness toward us in Christ Jesus." Your passion in life will be to worship the triune God.

Christians ought to be able to say that it is like a dream to be released from the control and power of Satan. The child of God is free to worship God throughout eternity.

Preparation for Heavenly Worship

Freedom in Christ is often misinterpreted, because self importance still tries to persuade the Christian to think in terms of "my individual freedom." The Psalmist, along with the whole counsel of God, talks about the freedom of the whole Old Testament Church.

For Christians, the concept of freedom in Christ is never an individualistic, private concern. Freedom in Christ is for the covenant community. It should be noted that the Psalmist speaks in the first person plural and uses plural pronouns:

> *We* were like those who dream
> *Our* mouth was filled with laughter
> *Our* tongue with singing
>   are glad.
> (Psalm 126:1-3)

He did not say "my" mouth, "my" tongue, or "my" joy. God "raised us up together, and made us sit together in the heavenly places in Christ Jesus" (Ephesians 2:6). Our relationship with God is not merely a private matter, nor is our worship individualistic and private.

The church never had to reckon with individualism until about two hundred years ago. Unfortunately individualism is the culprit undermining the church in this country. The covenant members of the church ought to pray as the Psalmist: "Bring back our captivity, O Lord, As the streams in the South" (Psalm 126:4).

It is important to remember the oppression and pain of the captivity. Christians have to recall what the Lord has done in the past so they can have joyful expectation of the future. When God's people are afflicted and oppressed there is consolation in remembering the gracious hand of the Lord.

Just as the Lord has appointed harvest to follow the planting of seeds, so He has appointed the consolation of His church to follow after their afflictions. While the church may face adversity, pain, suffering and distress, Christians must not think that it will last forever. It is those who are without Christ that will most certainly suffer affliction throughout all eternity.

God's people may find sorrow in their sowing, yet they will find joy in their reaping. This agricultural metaphor is meaningful indeed. For example, in the spring of the year people are busy planting vegetable gardens. They labor tilling the ground and drop the seed in the ground. Along with that labor and planting is hope; hope that it will turn into a plant and finally produce vegetables. Planting is not necessarily the joyful time. Planting is a time of hard work, toil, and as the Psalmist says, "we sow in tears" (Psalm 126:5).

However, painful work often finds pleasant rewards. It is the harvest time that brings joy. There is no longer any reason to doubt. The fruit of the sowing has paid off. Your handful of seed shall be greatly multiplied, so that many sheaves come from the seed. This simple agricultural metaphor reminds the church of God's power to turn sorrow into joy.

One of the reasons the church assembles to worship the true and living God is so the sorrow of laboring in this sinful world will turn into joy. When Christians gather to worship the Lord, they expect the Lord to reveal Himself. It is the joy they experience when God reveals Himself. The Lord has done great things by making Himself known to His church.

Preparation for heavenly worship must be accompanied by the joy of God's revelation. This raises more questions. Has God revealed Himself to you? Does God reveal Himself in creation? Does God reveal Himself in Scripture? When God does reveal Himself does it bring sadness or joy? Do you love to hear and embrace God's truth, even if it is painful? The pain of God's revelation is only temporary to the child of God. It is the joy of God's revelation that remains throughout all eternity.

The church still labors as God promises to fulfill His promise to His people. Remain faithful even when Satan's lies seem convincing. The church will find her joy as:

> Those who sow in tears
> Shall reap in joy.
> He who continually goes forth weeping
> Bearing seed for sowing,
> Shall doubtless come again with rejoicing,
> Bringing his sheaves with him.
> (Psalm 126:5-6)

An incredible act of God's grace is the gathering of God's church for worship. It is like a wonderful dream. Come to worship rejoicing so that even the heathens take notice of God's people in worship.

13. Worship by Divine Favor

Psalm 127

The western world is on the brink of intellectual bankruptcy. Martin Murphy wrote a book entitled, My *Christian Apology*. His argument is that the western world is in a state of "skeptical neutrality." The result is we have a "truth neutral culture." There is no metaphysic and neutrality has been crowned king. It opens the door for the invasion of skepticism in the entire cultural milieu. Christians tried to develop a "Christian sub-culture" to avoid the hard work of defending the faith. The abandonment of truth has an exponential affect on the doctrine of Scripture.

In his book, *The Passion of the Western Mind*, Richard Tarnas makes an astute observation about the nature of truth at the beginning of the 21st century. "The critical search for truth is constrained to be tolerant of ambiguity and pluralism, and its outcome will necessarily be knowledge that is relative and fallible rather than absolute or certain" (*The Passion of the Western Mind*, by Richard Tarnas, p. 396).

It is time for Christians to come out of their sub-culture, roll up their sleeves and rediscover the absolute infallible truth found in the Word of God. The central purpose of God's church is to offer worship according to His Word and for His glory. Three thousand years ago the Old Testament congregation went to Jerusalem to worship. They went there because God established it as the central place to worship. God's people did not view God's Word as relative and fallible, but rather absolute and infallible. It was in Jerusalem that the Old Testament saints would come to worship the name of God. You might say that Jerusalem was the cosmic center point for all worship. It was the time and place in which the Old Testament saint participated in a unique intense worship experience.

Today New Testament saints no longer make that journey to Jerusalem several times each year. Jesus told the Samaritan woman "that an hour is coming when neither in this mountain nor in Jerusalem shall you worship the Father." Jesus went on to say "that an hour is coming and now is when the true worshipers shall worship the Father in spirit and truth; for such people the Father seeks to be His worshipers" (John. 4:21ff).

New Testament saints may have that unique intense worship experience anyplace anytime because the Spirit of God manifests Himself more fully to believers in this age and apart from the Old Testament ceremonial laws. Worship privately at home and worship with family, but Christians may not entertain the idea that corporate collective worship is not necessary.

The visible Church is the agency for gathering and perfecting the saints that belong to the invisible Church. Therefore the visible Church is responsible for manifesting the invisible Church. The Church has the unique responsibility to maintain the sacred Scriptures, the Sacraments and public worship "for the gathering and perfecting of the saints, in this life, to the end of the world" (*Westminster Confession of Faith*, Chapter 25, Section 3).

God's people must assemble themselves to worship the true and living God. However, they must not assemble to be entertained. When they do assemble there must be the true preaching of the Word of God and the ordinances must be properly administered. Worship must be offered according to the Word of God.

The emphasis is on God. To participate in God-made, God-centered worship is a religious experience incomparable to any human invention, because true worship is by divine favor. Psalm 127 reveals that worship is by divine favor. The Psalmist uses the metaphors of God's creational ordinances to show His divine favor. Work, family, and worship are the creational ordinances relative to this Psalm. The fundamental lesson from it is that the pilgrim offers divine worship because of God's divine favor.

Worship by Divine Favor

The futility of human effort is so obvious in this Psalm, yet human effort is absolutely necessary. It only sounds contradictory to say that human effort is futile, but human effort is necessary. It may be an antinomy and may appear mysterious but, it is not contradictory. The necessity of human effort in the ministry of the church is an irrefutable biblical concept. "And He gave some as apostles, and some as prophets, and some as evangelists, and some as pastors and teachers, for the equipping of the saints for the work of service, to the building up of the body of Christ" (Ephesians 4:11-12). Jesus said, "Go therefore and make disciples of all the nations" (Matthew 28:19). The Bible indicates that human effort is absolutely necessary. Yet Psalm 127 states that human effort is vanity.

> They labor in vain (Psalm 127:1)
> The watchman stays awake in vain (Psalm 127:1)
> It is in vain to rise up early (Psalm 127:2)
> It is vain to sit up late, (Psalm 127:2)
> It is vain to eat the bread of sorrows. (Psalm 127:2)

The Psalmist refers to the vanity of human effort in these wisdom metaphors. First the Psalmist says, "Unless the Lord builds the house, they labor in vain who built it." There is every reason to believe that Solomon wrote this Psalm because it describes the human desire of David who wanted to build the temple, but the Lord would not allow it. Solomon not only realized his father's human inability to build the temple, he realized his own inability apart from the sovereign hand of God. Solomon's prayer after the building of the Temple reveals the sovereign hand of God in the planning, preparation and completion of the Temple. Solomon said, "You have kept what You promised Your servant David my father; You have both spoken with your mouth and fulfilled it with you hand, as it is this day" (2 Chronicles 6:15). Human effort alone will not build the kingdom of God.

Then you have the watchman who stays awake in vain. This refers to the guards who stood watch for the city. They were responsible for warning the king if a stranger or the enemy approached the city. Some of the prophets were called God's watchmen. The watchmen had a responsible position to warn and protect, but the guard is a mere man.

The Psalmist also mentions the vanity of rising up early and sitting up late and vainly eating the bread of sorrows. This is an indictment against working tirelessly to acquire the things of this world. Human labor is good and necessary, but without God it is miserable service and brings no moral satisfaction to the soul. The "bread of sorrows" is a figure of speech. In the context of this Psalm it may refer to the effort put into acquiring food for the table with anxiety, distress, and worry that the food may not be available. The operative word is "worry." The Lord Jesus Christ said, "do not worry about your life" (Matthew 6:25-34). If you devote your life to your own earthly endeavors, for your own glory, in the end it will be in vain.

The tower built in the land of Shinar, commonly called the tower of Babel, is a good example of laboring in vain. The people set out to build a tower "whose top is in the heavens." It was a futile attempt to worship the work of their hands (Isaiah 2:8). The Lord caused them to speak in an unknown tongue, which is often a sign of God's judgment. The impregnable Jericho was a human monument of failure. The best summary of this doctrine comes from the Lord of hosts: "They may build, but I will throw down" (Malachi 1:4). If God does not crown our efforts, our best laid plans are sure to fail.

This does not mean that Christians are not to work hard six days a week. This Psalm does not militate against that Christian work ethic. Work was a creation ordinance, therefore work is honorable. The Bible commands Christians to labor and do all their work in six days. God's Law is very clear; "Six days you shall labor and do all your work" (Exodus 20:8). Active in the affairs of our business is a Christian habit to be desired.

However, to keep this in perspective, "what profit is it to a man if he gains the whole world, and is himself destroyed or lost" (Luke 9:25)?

Work may be selfish and disregard the Lord God Sovereign or work may be for the glory of God. Without the grace of God labor is the product of wicked motives. It is the grace of God that turns work into joy (Proverbs 10:16). This principle applies to worship as well as work.

The created world and all that is in it is absolutely dependent on the independent Being that created everything. More importantly people are totally and in every way dependent on Him for eternal life. God is sovereign, independent and infinitely interested in the estate of every one of His children. God knows the pain, suffering and laborious life of His children "so He gives His beloved sleep" (Psalm 127:2). The Lord will give sleep to His beloved without anxiety. They do not fret about their estate when they awaken. Where the unbeliever labors to make His mark in this world, the believer puts his or her trust wholly in the Lord for all things in this life and the life to come.

The believer is content with his estate of providence. The world gives the unbeliever power, wealth, prestige, and temporal prominence. The grace of God gives the believer rest from the cares and sorrows of this world. It is God that gives rest and comfort so that His children will be alert and ready to worship Him. This doctrine from Holy Scripture is most important to God's people because they worship by divine favor. They are not distracted by the desires and cares of this world.

The believer sees God-centered worship as a time to behold the beauty of the Lord. The mind is stimulated by truth. The emotions are radically affected. The will is inclined to love God with rational comprehension and empirical expressions of joy. It is God's grace that enables the worshiper to see the full expression of God's character.

Divine favor is necessary, not only for worship, but for life itself. The Psalmist illustrates that by bringing the creational ordinance known as the family into the picture. The family is a gift from God. "Children are a heritage from the Lord, the fruit of the womb is a reward" (Psalm 127:3). It is the swelling of pride to talk of reproductive ability of the human race. The Hebrew word translated "heritage" literally refers to an inheritance that comes from Yahweh. Children are a gift from God, not the masterful work of two human beings. The Psalmist brings this creational ordinance before the people to remind them that God's divine favor is necessary for life.

God's people must trust God and submit to his divine law. They must ascribe to Him all honor, dignity and glory. When Christians come to understand that their very existence is a matter of divine favor, worship will be God-centered and heavenly focused.

Jesus said, "I am the vine, you are the branches. He who abides in me bears much fruit, for without me you can do nothing" (John 15:5). Salvation is a gift from Christ which He earned for all those who belong to the Lord. This Psalm uniquely drives the worshiping church to the cross of Christ. It shows Christians the helplessness of their sinful condition and that the only way of salvation is in Christ and Him alone. Then the people of God gather to worship by divine favor.

Now ask yourself these questions. Do I worship according to my own selfish motivations? Are my own human efforts at the center of worship, or do I worship by divine favor? Only you can answer those questions!

14. Fear and Blessing in Worship

Psalm 128

Biblical worship is not simply showing up for church on Sunday morning for one hour. Biblical worship is an act of the fullness of human capacity.

It is the responsibility of the church leaders to insure that the people of God gather to worship. Public worship is a collective activity. Worship is not merely individual and passive. It is corporate and active.

It is popular for some evangelical leaders to programize the congregation. It is the responsibility of the pastor to lead the congregation in worship, not in programs. It is the responsibility of the congregation to worship the Lord, not themselves. Programs, testimonies, and other such activities are for another place and time.

> When God's people assemble for worship they enter into the place where God dwells. God meets them, and they meet God. They find themselves face to face with none other than God Himself. Their worship is an intimate transaction between them and their God. If the church were full conscious of that truth, what dignity and reverence would characterize its worship! Of levity and frivolity there would not be a trace." (*The Glorious Body of Christ*, by R. B. Kuiper, p.347)

Adoration of God is the primary purpose and duty in worship. There is no hint in Scripture that man is to be adored in worship. How has the church moved so far off course? The answer is simple. Seminary professors are producing men who have exchanged the truth for a lie. God is the object of our attention. The lie is from the father of lies: "did God really mean…."

Until the church recovers a passion for God as the object of worship, the church will reap the lies of a man-centered ministry. Christians should cry out like the Psalmist. "O God, you are my God, early will I seek You; My soul thirsts for You; My flesh longs for You so I have looked for You in the sanctuary, to see Your power and your glory" (Psalm 63:1).

In Psalm 66:1-4a the extent of worship universally applies to the human race. "Make a joyful shout to God, all the earth! Sing out the honor of His name; Make His praise glorious. Say to God, How awesome are Your works! Through the greatness of Your power Your enemies shall submit themselves to You. All the earth shall worship You" (Psalm 66:1-4a). The word worship is derived from the Hebrew word *shachah* which literally means to bow down. The sin nature is an obstruction to godly worship, because the sin nature does not bow in humility.

To capture the meaning of "bow down in humble worship" imagine, just for a moment, that you are walking in the shoes of the Israelite, as he walks to Mount Zion to worship. Your and your travelling companions would sing all the way. "Blessed is every one who fears the Lord, Who walks in His ways" (Psalm 128:1). The Psalmist summarizes two necessary conditions for worship. The conditions are represented by the nature of the relationship to God. Odd as it may seem to modern day Christians, fear is a necessary condition for worship. Obedience is another condition necessary for worship.

Fear is innate to all human beings. God created everyone with the built-in disposition known as fear. Fear fills two primary functions. First, it is like a warning device. It warns every rational being that something may be wrong. Fear is most useful because it allows for preparation when there is the threat of danger. Fear also reminds dependent creatures that there is an independent God. Fear is the media that provokes terror or stimulates respect and reverence. Fear is either your ally or it is your enemy. If the negative side of fear, such as terror and guilt prevails, it will cause misery and trepidation to the soul. If the positive side, such as respect and reverence prevails, the soul will have comfort and peace.

The fear of the Lord establishes the greatness of God and the smallness of man. There is a great contrast between a holy God and sinful man. To dismiss preaching and teaching the doctrine of fear tends to incline man to think of himself as high up. It leads to the mistaken notion that God is **required** to show love, mercy, and grace. Without the fear of God justice will not find its proper place in life.

Sometimes the child of God may become overwhelmed with the threat of danger. The Israelites were often victims of that kind of fear. Fear must have the proper object. To understand the goodness of fear you must keep singing, "Blessed is every one who fears the Lord, Who walks in His ways" (Psalm 128:1).

Singing and preaching about fear is not popular in the modern contemporary church worship service. Even so, Christians are commanded to fear God. "And does not fear those who kill the body but cannot kill the soul. But rather fear Him who is able to destroy both soul and body in hell" (Matthew 10:28). Fear is an imperative verb. Therefore Christians are commanded to fear God. Fear is a biblical concept that Christians ought to desire. There are many benefits for those that fear the Lord.

> "The fear of the Lord is the beginning of knowledge" (Proverbs 1:7).
>
> "The fear of the Lord prolongs days" (Proverbs 10:27).
> "by the fear of the Lord one departs from evil" (Proverbs 16:6).
>
> "Blessed is the man who fears the Lord" (Psalm 112:1).

The fear of the Lord is necessary for acceptable worship. If you believe in the regulative principle of worship, then you believe that God commands the way to worship Him in the Word of God. The necessary objective prescription to worship is found in His Word.

Godly fear of God's Word is necessary to worship according to His Word. "But on this one will I look: On him who is poor and of a contrite spirit, and who trembles at My word" (Isaiah 66:2). The word tremble is akin to fear, but has a stronger sense. It literally means to be terrified. In simple terms God is incapable of a lie. Therefore, God's Word is the testimony of His covenant promises.

Since the only way to know how to worship God is from His Word, the fear of His Word will lead to worship which is pleasing to God. The Bible explains: "Fear God and give glory to Him, for the hour of His judgment has come; and worship Him who made heaven and earth, the sea and springs of water" (Revelation 14:7). The Psalmist summarizes this in one verse. "God is greatly to be feared in the assembly of the saints, and to be held in reverence by all those around Him" (Psalm 89:7).

The saints of God are blessed when they fear the Lord and walk in His ways. Obedience represents the love one has for the fearful God. The doctrine of Christian obedience is not limited to the Ten Commandments. The doctrine of obedience calls Christians to bring "every thought into captivity to the obedience of Christ" (2 Corinthians 10:5). It will take serious inquiry into the Word of God to bring every thought into captivity to the obedience of Christ. If you believe this portion of God's Word, then everything you do, say, or think ought to be supported by the Word of God.

Fear is necessary for a good relationship with God which always leads to worship in the fullest sense of the word. This Psalm of Ascent also brings a full orbed view of worship to the modern church. The Psalmist is persistent about the fullness of worship by bringing the creational ordinances into the picture.

Fear and Blessing in Worship

"The labor of your hands" is a form of worship (Psalm 128:2). God put Adam in the Garden of Eden and instructed Adam to "tend the garden and keep it" (Genesis 2:15). Work is a form of worship that leads to contentment and well being, only when it is done in the fear of the Lord.

God's blessing does not come to an idle, frivolous, and wasteful life. On the contrary, God's blessing comes to those who are useful, productive and happy in the calling to which God has called them. God's children serve (or work for) the Lord whatever their call is in life. When Christians serve the Lord, they also worship the Lord, because service or work and worship are bound together in God's covenant.

The Psalmist also calls our attention to another creation covenant, often referred to as marriage and the family. Marriage and family is God's blessing to those who fear the Lord. There is a slight shift in the use of the Hebrew words translated blessed in verses one and four. The blessedness in verse one stresses the positive effort of man. The blessedness in verse one comes because the man submits himself to the authority and sovereignty of God. The blessedness in verse four comes from God in the way of God's special presence, God's special grace, and God's keeping power. Any man who has God's blessing for marriage and family is the man who fears the Lord.

Christians worship God by serving Him in their vocations. They worship God through the blessing of the family. They also worship God collectively on the day He has appointed according to His Word. Vocations and families are temporary. Jobs and families will cease. However, worship to God by His elect people will be offered throughout eternity. This is the collective worship offered by God's covenant people.

The Psalmist says, "the Lord bless you out of Zion" (Psalm 128:5). "Out of" is an archaic expression referring to the source or origin of the blessing. It is from Zion or you might say it was from the holy place that God's people expected a blessing when they worshipped together in Jerusalem.

In this day and age we gather together on Sunday morning and Sunday evening to bow down before the Lord our God. We too expect a blessing from Zion - that is the heavenly Zion. The blessing we receive from worship is not temporary. Our blessing from worship has eternal consequences.

The Psalmist says if God blesses you from His heavenly home, it will affect you all the days of your life, even extending to your children's children. This is a metaphor that refers to an endless blessing.

In his book *Religious Affections* Jonathan Edwards made a comment worthy of the attention of the evangelical church of the 21st century. "Religious fear and hope are, once and again, joined together as jointly constituting the character of the true saints" (*The Rational Biblical Theology of Jonathan Edwards*, vol. 1, p. 331). Edwards then quotes the Word to prove his comment. "The Lord takes pleasure in those who fear Him, in those who hope in His mercy" (Psalm 147:11). "Behold, the eye of the Lord is on those who fear Him, on those who hope in His mercy" (Psalm 33:18).

No fear of God means there is no blessing from God. If there is no blessing from God there is no acceptable worship. God's blessing is the capstone of true worship. For that reason the Word of God issues a promise. "He will bless those who fear the Lord, both small and great" (Psalm 115:13).

Fear of the Lord will not only secure God's blessing, it

15. The Redeemed Suffering Church

Psalm 129

The word "redeem" may mean different things to different people, so I want to clarify the meaning of the word "redeemed" relative to the redeemed suffering church. Redeem is often used to refer to regaining possession something. For instance, under the Old Testament Levitical laws, the people of God were allowed to redeem property (Leviticus chapter 27). Redeem is also relative to honoring a promise. For instance, in Micah the promise to the Israelites was "the Lord will redeem you from the hand of your enemies" (Micah 4:10). Therefore the word "redeem" refers, in some sense, to God's covenant promise to save His people and to forgive their sins.

In the very height of suffering, the prophet Jeremiah expresses the redemptive covenant of God.

> Hear the word of the Lord, O nations, and declare it in the isles afar off." God will demonstrate His redemptive power in such a way that it will astonish all the nations of the earth. The announcement was remarkable. "He who scattered Israel will gather him, and keep him as a shepherd does his flock, For the Lord has redeemed Jacob, and ransomed him from the hand of one stronger than he. (Jeremiah 31:10-11)

This prophecy of Jeremiah promises that the Old Testament church will be restored by the generous hand of the Lord. At the time of his prophecy many if not most of the worshiping Israelites had been taken to Babylon as slaves. What does Jeremiah's prophecy mean for New Testament Christians? What does it mean to the local church? What does it mean to you personally?

God's generous hand of redemption means that God's people are in a distinctive favorable relationship with God. First it applies to individuals and then particular churches and ultimately the redeemed universal church. Those who were once under the power and control of Satan have been set free to worship the true and living God. God's promise for the people of God is that they will be restored into the hand of the Lord in due time. They will be redeemed by the Lord.

The Redeemed Suffering Church may sound conflicting. It is not inharmonious or contradictory. Although the church is redeemed in a legal sense, it is suffering in the moral sense. Christians suffer because of sin. The enemies of God are the enemies of Christians (Psalm 37:20). Jeremiah was a man of exceptional courage in the face of severe opposition from the enemies of God. In one of Jeremiah's prayers he prayed:

> Let them be ashamed who persecute me,
> But do not let me be put to shame;
> Let them be dismayed,
> But do not let me be dismayed.
> Bring on them the day of doom,
> And destroy them with double destruction
> (Jeremiah 17:18).

Those words may sound a little harsh, but they were inspired by God. It is an imprecatory prayer. It is a prayer that appeals to God's justice. If a person is in a right relationship with God then there is no concern about being destroyed.

Some Christians claim these imprecatory prayers are not for the church today. Imprecatory prayers are said to be too wrathful for a loving God. Others simply say they are too hard to understand. The imprecatory prayers in the Bible, of which there are many, have not been abrogated. They are petitions made to God and Christians appeal to God as He alone can exercise His love, kindness, judgment, and righteousness on earth.

The Redeemed Suffering Church

Jesus taught His disciples saying, "to love your enemies and do good to those that persecute you" (Matthew 6:43-48; Luke 6:27-36). This doctrine teaches Christians not to seek revenge when they are wronged. It is not for the Christian to execute judgment, but Christians ought to pray that God will execute judgment.

The church is redeemed in the sense that God will ultimately save the elect because His covenant to save them is fulfilled in the ministry of the Lord Jesus Christ. Yet God's children suffer; they suffer at the hands of the enemy of the church. God's children suffer because the enemies of God are unable get their hands on God.

Psalm 129 describes the redeemed suffering church. Worship is the general theme of the Psalms of Ascent, but each Psalm expresses a unique dimension of worship. Each Psalm brings us closer and closer to the holy place of God's special presence.

In anticipation of appearing before God, the Psalmist reminds God's people of the suffering of the redeemed worshiper. "Many a time they have afflicted me from my youth, Let Israel now say many a time they have afflicted me from my youth; Yet they have not prevailed against me" (Psalm 129:1-2).

Notice the shift from the individual to the whole church. Christians stand as individuals before God, but they all worship collectively as a whole church. The biblical doctrine of worship calls for unity in the congregation. When the Apostle Paul learned that there were contentions (quarrels) among the individual churchmen at Corinth the apostle demanded unity. Paul expected the church to speak the same thing, and that there should not be any divisions in the church. The individual church members were saying "I am of Paul" or "I am of Apollos" or "I am of Cephas" or "I am of Christ." Then Paul asked the question: "Is Christ divided?" The answer is no and neither can the church be divided, except at the hand of the enemy of God (See 1 Corinthians 3:1-4). God's redeemed worshipers suffer when there is division in the church. Many local churches have experienced division because the enemies of God stir up strife.

The suffering of the redeemed worshiper is severe indeed as the Psalmist describes by a figure of speech. "The plowers plowed on my back; they made their furrows long" (Psalm 129:3). This agricultural metaphor describes the pain and oppression of an individual, yet its application is to the whole church. This is a picture of the harsh punishment of a whipping that rips the flesh apart.

The redeemed worshiper may suffer in this world, but time in this world is infinitesimal compared to the life in the world to come. The suffering redeemed worshiper must keep his mind on the holy place of God's special presence in the New Heavens and the New Earth. The present suffering of the redeemed worshiper must not overshadow the joy of the redeemed worshiper in the heavenly church.

The righteousness of God is the joy of the suffering worshiper. "The Lord is righteous; he has cut in pieces the cords of the wicked" (Psalm 129:4). God promises to put an end to the tyranny and domination of the wicked. Many times Christians are not able to see the hand of the Lord at work, but they must remember, as the Psalmist says, "The Lord is righteous." He is just and justice will prevail over those who persecute God's people.

When Christians are persecuted they may be tempted to question God's justice. A biblical understanding of God's justice will help avoid the temptation. Justice is God's upright character and integrity demonstrated by his correct judgment because of His holiness. The present judicial system in this country has made such a mockery of justice that most people have simply lost sight of the meaning of justice. Jonathan Edwards said, "It is another mystery of providence, that God suffers so much public injustice to take place in the world" (*Works of Jonathan Edwards*, Yale Edition, vol. 14, p. 536). The mystery of injustice is reason enough to pray for the vindication of God's justice.

Justice is not a pleasant thought to the unbeliever, because justice means that one gets what one deserves. The unbeliever and believer alike deserve God's eternal wrath and punishment. The unbeliever gets what he or she deserves, but God shows mercy to the believer. The sins of the believer are still punished in Jesus Christ thus showing the justice of God.

The redeemed worshiper will experience joy knowing that justice will prevail and to put it into psychological terms, God will take care of His own. "For thus says the Lord of hosts; He sent Me after glory, to the nations which plunder you; for he who touches you touches the apple of His eye" (Zechariah 2:8). Charles Spurgeon has said, "The shortest way to ruin is to meddle with a saint." The joy of the redeemed worshiper is that God's justice will prevail.

The redeemed suffering worshiper must be patient and pray. The song of the Psalmist was really a prayer. "Let those who hate Zion be put to shame and turned back. Let them be as the grass on the housetops, which withers before it grows up" (Psalm 129:5-6). This is not a prayer of hatred and bitterness. It is a prayer to honor the character and essence of God. It is a prayer for the vindication of the righteousness of God. It is a prayer with confidence to a sovereign God.

Many professing Christians have heard or will hear the words, "Let all those who hate Zion be put to shame and turned back" and think that it is an isolated reference in Scripture. Consult the full counsel of God and you will find the Bible has much more to say about the wrath of God than the love of God. Imprecatory prayers may sound difficult to you, but they remain a part of God's infallible word and Christians must believe God gave them for their own good and God's glory.

Another imprecatory Psalm will bring this concept into focus.

> Let those be put to shame and brought to dishonor who seek after my life; Let those be turned back and brought

to confusion who plot my hurt. Let them be like chaff before the wind, and let the angel of the Lord chase them. Let their way be dark and slippery, and let the angel of the Lord pursue them. For without cause they have hidden their net for me in a pit, which they have dug without cause for my life. (Psalm 35:4-7)

Those unnamed men in this Psalm who are seeking to destroy David are ungodly men. Ungodly men are enemies of God.

John Calvin believed that when the ungodly gird and prepare themselves for destroying the Church, they are usually inflated with intolerable pride. Pride is a root sin and David is praying that the identifying marks will bring them to repentance. The goal of this prayer is not destruction, but repentance.

The Psalmist prays for several specific things to happen to the impenitent sinner. First, he prays for them to be ashamed. Shame is an emotional response that comes from some dishonorable or wicked behavior. The Lord alone has the right to shame the wicked man, but we all have the responsibility to pray that the righteousness of God will be vindicated. Then the Psalmist prays that his enemies will be brought to a state of confusion. Again the Psalmist calls for the Lord to avenge the worshiper. Christians have to be careful when they pray imprecatory prayers, so that they are not prejudiced. It is not a prayer of retaliation because the Lord says "Vengeance is Mine, I will repay" (Hebrews 10:30).

These imprecatory prayers are made to God and Christians appeal to God as He alone can exercise His love, kindness, judgment, and righteousness on earth. They must pray these prayers as if though Christ Himself were praying them, because ultimately if they are heard in the heavenly courts, they must be mediated by Christ Himself.

A friend told me about a vow he made during his ordination service. I wrote it down and would like to share it with you. He said, "Lord, make me a watchman, as the prophets of old, to warn not only myself, but the whole church of the judgments of God and boldly declare the saving grace of Jesus Christ for the salvation of men, women, boys and girls."

Are the people of God being warned of the judgments of God? Do they understand the justice of God that will prevail in the end? If so, the saving grace of Jesus Christ ought to be declared for the salvation of the soul.

Christ understands the redeemed suffering church and gives His blessing to the redeemed suffering church.

16. The Redeemed Worshiping Church

Psalm 130

The redeemed church consists of all those that belong to God. The redeemed church has three dimensions. The first is the church in the past consisting of all the redeemed beginning with Adam up until the last person that went to be with the Lord. The second dimension is the church in the present time. It consists of all God's people who are alive today. Finally there is the church of the future. It consists of all those yet to be born who will be redeemed by Christ.

The redeemed worshiping Church in the present time has distinctive marks. The first is an understanding of God's will for those who worship. The essential nature of the church is that God's people belong to it. Although there are many members in the church with different gifts, every member individually and the church collectively have one purpose. The purpose of the church is to worship God.

The church has a mission and a ministry. The mission includes evangelism. The ministry includes teaching and fellowship. The church is responsible to engage in the great cultural mandate, minister to its members, but its purpose is singular. It is to worship God.

There is true worship and false worship. True worship is designed by the Lord. It is the responsibility of the church to carry out God's design. How do Christians know what the Lord desires in worship? It is found in His Word. The redeemed worshiper says, "I wait for the Lord, my soul waits, and in His word I do hope" (Psalm 130:5). The word hope in that context does not refer to wishful thinking. The mundane use of the word "hope" in our culture most often refers to a dream come true against the odds. The biblical use of the word "hope" in this context is to trust in the object of hope which in this case is the

Word of God. The ultimate trust of the redeemed worshiper is the Lord. "For You are my hope, O Lord God; You are my trust from my youth" (Psalm 71:5).

The Psalmist connects hope with patience. "I wait for the Lord, my soul waits" (Psalm 130:5). Waiting on the Lord is not natural to man, yet Christians demonstrate this virtue because of God's supernatural grace. Waiting on the Lord is evidence of a lively faith.

The Psalmist emphasizes the need to wait upon the Lord. This particular doctrine is often abused by professing Christians. To wait upon the Lord does not mean to live an idle life. "If anyone will not work, neither shall he eat" (Thessalonians 3:10). The illustration used by the Psalmist shows the need to be diligent and alert. "My soul waits for the Lord, my soul waits for the Lord more than those who watch for the morning – yes, more than those who watch for the morning" (Psalm 130:6).

The watchman was the man who guarded the city. He was alert and busy guarding the city. The Psalmist says, "my soul waits for the Lord" and then compares his waiting to the busy watchman. Waiting on the Lord refers to the perseverance and un-mitigating resolve to trust the promises of God. It may sound like a paradox, but a Christian that waits on the Lord is actually a busy Christian.

This is especially important for the redeemed worshiper. Christians ought to delight in God's design for worship. The Word of God, singing Psalms and hymns, tithes and offerings, baptism, the Lord's Supper, prayer and the benediction is God's design for worship. If that sounds simple or boring, then, "wait upon the Lord and hope in His Word." Christians worship because they love the object of their worship, God the father, God the Son, and God the Holy Spirit.

Probably the best way for each individual Christian to own this doctrine is to put it in the first person singular. "In His Word I do hope" because sin is waiting at the door to overtake me.

Another distinctive mark of the redeemed worshiping church is the conviction of sin. "If you, Lord, should mark iniquities, who could stand" (Psalm 130:3). This verse describes the condition of the human race. In Paul's letter to the Romans he expresses the same doctrine in different terms; "for all have sinned and fall short of the glory of God" (Romans 3:23). An understanding of the doctrine of sin is necessary to understand the conviction of sin. Sin is the lack of absolute righteousness and perfection of all God's commandments. Any serious study of the Bible will reveal that God has given hundreds of commandments, both moral and reasonable. Evidence and common sense reveals that no man or woman can keep those commandments fully and perfectly.

Total depravity is a concept that explains the biblical doctrine of sin. The word depravity refers to corruption, so total depravity refers to the total corruption of man, both body and soul. Total depravity is an appropriate concept because it brings the totality of human nature into the picture. It raises the question: Is human nature good or evil? Do people sin because they are sinners by nature or do they sin because of their social and environmental circumstances? If the latter, then that person may be able to save himself or herself from eternal damnation.

The definition of the biblical doctrine of sin includes "original sin" and "actual sins." Original sin is a biblical doctrine that refers to the place and the effect of the sin of our first parents, Adam and Eve. The place of original sin is in the total human being, both body and soul. The effect of original sin is the actual sins committed by every human being.

The guilt of Adam's sin, not his sin, is the natural state of man after the Fall. Guilt implies punishment. "Therefore, as through one man's offense judgment came to all men, resulting in condemnation" (Romans 5:18). The imputation [legal representation] of Adam's sin is often misunderstood. Please notice that "the guilt" of Adam's sin was imputed, not the sin itself. Francis Turretin gives a clear and brief, but definitive statement on guilt. Turretin explains that "Guilt is the obligation to punishment from previous sin" (*Institutes of Elenctic Theology*, by Francis Turretin, vol. 1, p. 594). Adam's sin was sufficient to require the condemnation of the entire human race. This doctrine explains that God's justice is absolute. Christ redeemed those whom God calls to Himself, which means that God's love is arbitrary.

The inescapable fact for all humanity is that God must be pressed out of the mind. The knowledge of God in the mind of men is the haunting punishment for the sin of idolatry. They do not prefer to think about the nature and character of God because they are reminded of the due punishment that will come from His hand. The way human beings cope with the due punishment is by diversions. Diversions are simply distractions. These diversions are the only relief available for the totally depraved mind. The godless state of mind is always in a state of stupor, confusion, and ever contradicting itself.

The answer to this problem of sin is not the eradication of sin. The answer is for the sinner to admit that he or she is a sinner. The answer is a change of the soul (mind, will, and emotions) by the power of the Holy Spirit. The mind must be renewed, not perfected. The will must be changed to desire good rather than evil. The emotions must take on a new face. The answer is to seek the Lord while He may be found. The answer is to hear the truth of God's saving grace. The answer is to pray that God may change the soul. The answer is to believe on the Lord Jesus Christ.

Actual sins proceed from original sin. Actual sins are those that God commands but Christians fail to obey either by commission or omission. The Ten Commandments are the reference point for obeying God's law, but there are hundreds of other commandments in the Bible. For instance, the Word of God commands Christians: "do not be conformed to this world" (Romans 12:2). Actual sins also include heart sins. For example, Jesus said, "I say to you that whoever is angry with his brother without a cause shall be in danger of the judgment" (Matthew 5:22).

Conviction of sin is not a popular subject in the modern evangelical redeemed worshiping church. Contrary to the Bible the most popular subjects among evangelicals are prosperity, love, and healing. God will not hear the prayer of the redeemed worshiper until he or she confesses his or her sin (original) and sins (actual). The passion of the soul expressed by the Psalmist ought to be the passion of the modern church. "Out of the depths I have cried to You, O Lord; Lord hear my voice! Let your ears be attentive to the voice of my supplications" (Psalm 130:1-2). The worshiper was aware of his condition before God.

There are several aspects to the confession of the redeemed worshiper. The depth of his sin, sorrow, misery, and guilt was great and he was nothing but a mere men. And even though God is absolute holy and perfect in being, he still cried out to the Lord God Almighty.

The redeemed worshiper cried out to God because he knew and believed that God could and would forgive his sin and sins. "But there is forgiveness with You, that You may be feared" (Psalm 130:4). In the darkest hour God still gives His people light. When doubt and despair antagonize the soul, there is one place to go and that is to the Lord.

The transcendence of God does not allow us to see the objective nature of His forgiveness. Scripture, however, teaches that a number of factors may affect divine forgiveness. God's divine forgiveness is not merely cause and effect. He is compassionate and understands our weaknesses. "As far as the east is from the west, so far has he removed our transgressions from us. . .for he knows how we are formed, he remembers that we are dust" (Psalm 103:12-14). God is also aware of our ignorance. Jesus said, "Father forgive them, for they do not know what they do" (Luke 23:34).

The presence of righteous men in a sinful society has some influence on the larger community. "Run to and fro through the streets of Jerusalem; see now and know; and seek in her open places if you can find a man, if there is anyone who executes judgment, who seeks the truth, and I will pardon her" (Jeremiah 5:1). God's goodness and love is a factor in His forgiveness. "For You, Lord, are good and ready to forgive and abundant in mercy to all those who call upon You" (Psalm 86:5). The redeemed worshiper ought to understand forgiveness from God's perspective. The result is that God will be feared, because God has revealed that He is just and will not overlook sins, but He is merciful and will forgive sins.

Conviction of sin leads to confession. Confession leads to confidence for the redeemed worshiper. Assurance of God's grace is the comfort Christians find from the Lord of mercy. "O Israel, hope in the Lord; for with the Lord there is mercy" (Psalm 130:7). There is an obvious shift from the individual to the church collectively. It makes perfectly good sense. The purpose of human existence is to worship the Lord. There is a great chasm between sinful man and holy God. The way to bridge the chasm is for sinful man to have a conviction of his sin and sins. He confesses them to a merciful God and there finds forgiveness and assurance.

The redeemed worshiping church is the place where the individual redeemed worshiper joins the company of God's people and worships collectively. The Psalmist proceeds on his way to be in the special presence of God in worship. He enters the holy place with confidence and joy.

The redeemed worshiping church is confident to appear before the Lord. The church worships "the Lord God, merciful and gracious, longsuffering, and abounding in goodness and truth, keeping mercy for thousands, forgiving iniquity and transgression and sin" (Exodus 34:6-7).

The redeemed worshiping church will find her own dignity when she waits upon the Lord and hopes in the Word of God. God reveals His mercy and love to His redeemed worshiping church.

The Redeemed Worshiping Church

The redeemed worshiping church is convicted of sin, confesses sin, and finds confidence in the Lord's forgiveness and redemption. Confession and confidence is still tainted with sin, yet the redeemed worshiping church will find hope in the Word of God. The Word of God promises great joy for the redeemed worshiping church.

17. God is the Center of Worship

Psalm 131

The Psalms of Ascent are richly adorned with themes of collective worship. They remind Christians of how far they are away from God in one sense, but in another sense they remind Christians of how close God comes when Christians gather to worship Him.

Unfortunately Christians often fail to worship the true and living God, the triune God, the all powerful, all knowing, and sovereign God according to His word. Worship in the modern church seems inclined toward self worship in a spirit of contradiction and confusion. Self worship began in the Garden of Eden when Adam and Eve desired their independence more than they desired to worship their Creator.

Since that time God's ways have been repulsive to Adam's progeny. Satan and his craft and charm are very much alive today. The trap that Christians fall into is similar to the question that Satan asked Eve, "Indeed, has God said… (Genesis 3:1)?" If a difficult doctrine comes into a discussion, you may hear someone say, "Did God really say that?" It is typical to resist the Word of God if the doctrine is found objectionable to the sinful human nature.

It ought to be the passion of every Christian to recover the biblical concepts of worship. The Psalms of Ascent is the story of the worshiper preparing to gather to worship with the congregation of God's people. To recover biblical worship, a study of the Psalms of Ascent will be a great aid. Each Psalm has its place in comforting, strengthening, preparing and gathering God's people for worship. Psalm 131 ends the long journey from the distant land of mescheh and kedar. After the threat of all the dangers of the trip, even death itself, the worshiper finds himself or herself safe in the compound of Mount Zion.

Imagine that you are one of those Old Testament worshipers. You have made a long difficult and dangerous trip to Jerusalem to worship God collectively with God's people. You know that God was gracious in providing all your needs and protecting you. How would you respond? What would be your first thought. Would you shout, sing or pray?

The first word out of David's mouth was "Lord." David appeals to his Creator and Redeeming Savior; the Lord who sustains provides and governs all His people and their actions. Worship begins with "Lord!" It is for that reason that many churches will have an invocation to begin the time of collective worship. The invocation is to call upon the Lord and remember that He is the object of worship. "Praise the Lord, call upon His name; Declare His deeds among the peoples, make mention that His name is exalted" (Isaiah 12:4). The invocation tells the worshiper to give all of his or her attention to the Lord.

A friend told me about a book he read entitled *O Come, Let us Worship*. He said it was written by a conservative evangelical minister. Early on in this book the writer asked the question "What is the answer to the problem of less than meaningful and satisfying experiences of corporate worship?" He gave several answers, none of which really answered the question. This Psalm answers the question with the first word – Lord.

Meaningful worship begins with God-centered worship. All rational creatures ponder the meaning of life. Some philosophers and theologians devote their full energy to discover the purpose of life. From the least to the greatest, they will discover that the meaning and purpose of life begins with the Lord.

Contrary to the world view commonly known as consumerism, all the satisfying experiences of life, including corporate worship, is a gift from God. The search for a satisfying experience in corporate worship tends to turn toward man-centered worship.

God is the Center of Worship

God-centered worship is necessary for a meaningful and satisfying experience in corporate worship. God-centered worship requires that Christians consult the Word of God to find out how He wants them to worship Him. It may sound trite, but the fundamental principle in this text is to look up and see the holiness and glory of God; then look down and see the condition of the sinful soul of man.

God's people, like David, must not come to worship God with a proud heart. The Psalmist looked up and down and then said, "Lord, my heart is not haughty" (Psalm 131:1). The Hebrew word translated "haughty" in the *New King James Bible* is a word that may also be translated "exalted." In Psalm 131 it certainly refers to pride. Pride is a condition of the heart that surfaces in words and actions. Pride is one of the primary reasons that people violate the Ten Commandments. It is impossible to put God first if pride is in the way. As the Bible says, "Before destruction the heart of a man is haughty" (Proverbs 18:12).

We see an example of the destructive power of pride in the life of the Old Testament King Uzziah. The Chronicler states it in these terms. "But when he (King Uzziah) was strong his heart was lifted up to his destruction for he transgressed against the Lord his God by entering the temple of the Lord to burn incense on the altar of incense" (2 Chronicles 26:16). King Uzziah's heart was filled with pride. King Uzziah's pride was destructive. This event takes place in the context of worship. This is another example of someone worshiping God the way they thought it ought to be rather than the way God prescribed in His Word. The priests warned King Uzziah, but he did not listen to them.

> Then Uzziah became furious; and he had a censer in his hand to burn incense. And while he was angry with the priests, leprosy broke out on his forehead, before the priests in the house of the Lord, beside the incense altar. And Azariah the chief priest and all the priests looked at

him, and there, on his forehead, he was leprous; so they thrust him out of that place. Indeed he also hurried to get out, because the Lord had struck him. King Uzziah was a leper until the day of his death. He dwelt in an isolated house, because he was a leper; for he was cut off from the house of the Lord. (2 Chronicles 26:19-21)

The danger of gathering to worship with pride in the heart may have horrible consequences. Uzziah lost the joy in worship because he offered worship not commanded by God. He lost the joy of gathering and worshiping with the people of God. Pride in the heart is a condition. Pride is innate. It is part of the sinful nature. Pride is incapable of worshiping a holy God. Pride demands competition, but pride cannot compare or compete with God. Pride says "get rid of God in worship" so "I" will get all the attention.

The Psalmist describes the expression of pride in terms of "lofty eyes" (Psalm 131:1). You will notice that the Psalmist moves from the inward condition of the heart to the outward expression of that inward condition. Arrogance is the word in modern times that best fits the "lofty eyes." Arrogance is an expression of the condition of the heart. The consequences of gathering to worship God with a prideful heart and an arrogant disposition are deadly.

A proud man thinks that he is exalted above others. One way to feed pride is to have an association with rank and authority and use it to elevate the ego. King David had a close relationship with God, even to the point that God spoke to David (See 2 Samuel 2:2; 2 Samuel 5:19; et al). Even though God spoke to David and treated David with exceeding grace and mercy, David did not let it turn into pride and arrogance. To the contrary David said, "Neither do I concern myself with great matters, nor the things too profound for me" (Psalm 131:1).

Some Christians want to know more about God and His created order than God has chosen to reveal. Christians must never seek to explore the secret will and mind of God. God's secret counsel is not a matter for our attention. God has revealed all that he wants us to know in the Word of God and natural revelation. To try to go further is blasphemy. God has revealed Himself to His people in the natural order of things and in the Word of God. For instance, God has revealed the law. It condemns the unconverted sinner. Then God reveals the gospel, which is the good news of God's saving grace. The converted sinner should then study the Word of God to know how to live in a sinful world. Inquiry into alleged secret knowledge was a feature of second and third century Gnosticism. It feeds the pride of a sinful soul and cuts off the grace of God.

This is particularly important in worship. The biblical design for Christian worship is not intellectual stimulation, although Christians must exercise the mind in order to worship. Worship is not the place to get a word from the Lord or moral lesson from the preacher. Worship is not the place to entertain theological or philosophical speculations or disputations. Worship is about giving, not getting! Worship is about God, not man. Every word and every action in worship is a body and soul response to the glory, honor, majesty and dignity of God.

True worship comes from a humble man who, like David, has an understanding of his sinful nature and the actual sins that proceed from that nature. In Psalm 51 you will find David's prayer, a prayer that reflects his sin nature from birth as well as an awareness of actual sins. David was aware that his sinful pride was an offense to a holy God.

Now for two exam questions about the nature of Christian worship. How can a sinful creature appear before a holy God? How can a sinful creature offer worship to a holy God?

First the sinful creature must see his sinful condition in comparison to a holy God. Then the sinful creature must be regenerated by the powerful work of the Holy Spirit. The converted sinful creature will find his or her fulfillment and satisfaction in the saving work of Jesus Christ.

The Psalmist explains this unique experience by using a metaphor of a weaned child. David said, "Surely I have calmed and quieted my soul, like a weaned child with his mother; like a weaned child is my soul within me" (Psalm 131:2). Before a child is weaned he or she must cry for milk and nourishment. A weaned child will have more confidence than the child that depends on mother for nourishment. As a weaned child he was mature and understood his limitations and God's goodness. The Psalmist found fulfillment, satisfaction, and contentment in worship, not because he was filled with pride, arrogance, and intellectual superiority, but he found contentment because his soul was like a weaned child. The content soul will worship with confidence and conviction that it is the Spirit of God working in him both to will and to do. The Psalmist expressed a meaningful and satisfying worship experience to the Lord like a child in the presence of God.

Is your corporate collective worship like that of the Psalmist? Do you have a meaningful and satisfying worship experience? Is it true worship or merely a psychological experience? If you say no, then you must seek the Lord your God for he who seeks finds and to him who knocks it will be opened. If you say yes, "I do have a meaningful and satisfying worship experience," then the Lord says to you, "O Israel, hope in the Lord from this time forth and forever" (Psalm 131:3).

The experience of one man translates to the whole congregation. Israel is a reference to the whole congregation of God's people. The worship experience of one person affects the many who join together in collective worship. Everyone must trust the Lord now and forever. John Calvin summarized this Psalm by saying, "Our hope is of the right kind when we cherish humble and sober views of ourselves, and neither wish nor attempt anything without the leading and approbation of God" (*Commentary on Psalms*, by John Calvin). Christians everywhere are called to worship with humility, respect, dignity, and reverence. O Israel, hope in the Lord.

18. Worship Coram Deo

Psalm 132

The worshiper is ready to join with God's other people for worship, *Coram Deo*. The Latin term *Coram Deo* literally means "before the face of God." The presence of God and His kingdom was essential to the Old Testament Congregation. Actually it is essential to the New Testament congregation.

Christians live and worship *Coram Deo* during this life and it will continue throughout eternity. God secures this special relationship with His covenant promises. A covenant is a solemn promise made by an oath. Sometimes the covenant is solemnized by a verbal formula or a symbolic action.

The kingdom of God is universal. The kingdom of God defines the ownership of God. The culture Christians live in is part of God's kingdom. The church they minister and worship in is part of God's kingdom.

This kingdom concept is not just a general concept. During formal worship the Old Testament saints regard the Lord as the King over the whole world, including the enemies of God. Although the whole world is under God's rule, he created and chose a people to be His special possession. They are called the covenant people of God.

God made a kingdom covenant with David that is recorded in 2 Samuel 7:1-16. God made four promises about His kingdom and His relationship with His people.

> "I will appoint a place for My people Israel, and will plant them that they may dwell in a place of their own and move no more" (2 Samuel 7:10).

> "Also the Lord tells you that He will make you a house" (2 Samuel 7:11).

"I will set up your seed after you, who will come from your body, and I will establish his kingdom" (2 Samuel 7:12).

"I will establish the throne of his kingdom forever" (2 Samuel 7:13).

The covenant God made with David through the prophet Nathan is called a kingdom covenant. God promised to establish the throne of David's kingdom forever and the seed would come from David's body. David's off-spring did rule in Israel until 586 B.C. Then the Babylonians sacked Jerusalem, destroyed the temple, and enslaved the king. David's dynasty was dethroned. So what about God's promise for an eternal kingdom?

God does not make frivolous promises. David wanted to build God a house - a house made of bricks, blocks, and wood. God had other plans. First, God must build man a house, a house not made with hands. It would be an eternal house for all of God's covenant people. God's eternal house is nothing more than a reference to the kingdom of Jesus Christ. David's eternal seed is Jesus Christ. The throne of the kingdom of Jesus Christ has been established forever. Jesus Christ is King of kings. Americans have been conditioned to reject authority and sovereignty, because democracy tends toward individualism and autonomy. Christians have a sovereign King, the Lord Jesus Christ, who has all authority to rule. The democratization of Christianity, has seriously defamed the royal office of Christ's kingship. Christ performs his work as the omnipotent and eternal King at the place He is located at this present time. It is the duty of Christians to behold Christ as the King of their lives. Christians use jargon such as "Christ is Lord" but they treat Him like He was their good buddy rather than the eternal governor of their soul.

The kingdom of God is not a private kingdom. It is made of God's people collectively. The kingdom of God is not a club and no monthly dues are necessary. God provides for His kingdom. The kingdom of God is not a society established for the well being of its residents. It is made up of God's elect from every nation and tribe on earth from all times past, present and yet to come. The kingdom of God is a spiritual kingdom, but it is prefigured in time and space and so God uses types and figures to represent the eternal kingdom to come. The kingdom of God is for God's people to enjoy now through worship, praise, and adoration.

In Psalm 132 and in 2 Samuel you will notice that David is the one disturbed about the dwelling place of the Lord. David said, "I will not go into the chamber of my house or go up to the comfort of my bed; I will not give sleep to my eyes or slumber to my eyelids, until I find a place for the Lord, A dwelling place for the Mighty One of Jacob" (Psalm 132:3-5).

David made a vow to the Lord. David's vow is an example of private worship. A lawful vow is part of divine worship and such a vow is made to God alone. Making a vow is a serious matter and subject to eternal consequences. "When you make a vow to God, do not delay to pay it; For He has no pleasure in fools" (Ecclesiastes 5:4). David's vow was concerned with the public worship of God and establishing true worship so all believers might prepare for the coming eternal Sabbath. David's interest was that he would not be happily settled in his house when the Lord's house was a temporary place of worship. It was a custom with the Puritans in New England to build the town meeting house as quickly as they built their own individual homes. The meeting house served as a place of worship. It was not called a church building, which is an anomaly, but rather a meeting house because that is where the church assembled for worship.

Private affairs such as having a nice home to live in is not nearly as important as the establishment of collective worship for God's children. This does not mean that Christians may not live in nice homes, but priorities are important as David demonstrated from this Psalm. Not only that, but collective worship is the starting point for all the injunctions we find in Scripture. Christians cannot expect to obey God at any point until they first understand their obligation to worship Him collectively.

Although the scholars are unsettled on the date of this Psalm, it was probably written by David or his son Solomon. The author of this Psalm reflected on worship during the period of the Judges. During the period of the Judges, worship was nothing more than a subjective religious experience. Individualism was the order of the day and outward forms of public worship were offered to false gods.

David worked for the reformation of worship. David would not rest until he found a place where God would visit and commune with His people. God's visitation was important and should be in the contemporary church. Unlike the feeble promises of men, God's promises stand.

Joy in worship is the result true worship. The Psalmist appeals to all believers with two challenges.

"Let us go into His tabernacle" (Psalm 132:7)
"Let us worship at His footstool" (Psalm 132:7)

The tabernacle was a symbol of the kingdom of God. The tabernacle eventually became the temple which housed the ark of the Lord. The temple and especially the ark symbolize the earthly rule of God. During the New Testament period, until the second coming of Christ, the church symbolizes God's rule on earth; The ark has been replaced by the final redemptive work of Jesus Christ and Christ is the head of the church.

If the Old Testament saints saw the necessity of gathering collectively to worship, how much more is required by the New Testament saints? This sobering question will cause all of God's people to lift up their minds and hearts in worship to the true and living God and use every ordinance God has given, so that He may be worshipped.

Worship Coram Deo

Do you want to worship, *Coram Deo*? If so, then God has some good news for you.

> For the Lord has chosen Zion; He has desired it for His dwelling place: This is my resting place forever; Here I will dwell, for I have desired it. I will abundantly bless her provision; I will satisfy her poor with bread, I will also clothe her priests with salvation, and her saints shall shout aloud for joy. (Psalm 132:13-16)

The Lord has chosen Zion is a work of God. "Her saints shall shout aloud for joy" is an expression of thanksgiving to God. The Old Testament Greek translation is "The Lord elected Zion." The words reflect the meaning of the text. The English word "elected" is translated from a Greek verb which means "God called out for himself." When God chooses, it's always the perfect choice. When people make a choice, it is often a bad choice. A very good reason for Christians to shout with joy is when they worship, *Coram Deo*.

It was God's choice that made Mount Zion special as a church underage. Jerusalem was no different, in a secular sense, than any other Canaanite town until God chose it and then dwelt there among His people.

It is God's choice that makes the church (GOD'S COVENANT PEOPLE) sacred and set apart. Let me repeat in a loud voice: A BUILDING OR ANY PHYSICAL STRUCTURE IS NOT THE CHURCH (capitalized for emphasis). It is the people of God that God has called to Himself that constitutes the church. God has chosen the church to worship Him. The church is different that any other institution, organization, or assembly of people on this earth, because all the clubs, institutions, and organizations on this earth will cease to exist, but the church is eternal.

It is not uncommon for a particular church to advertise, with great preponderance, that the goal of their particular church is evangelism. There are literally dozens of disciplines required of Christians through the ministry of the church. Evangelism is one among the many, but there is also discipleship, visit the sick, feed the poor, and many more.

God promised to prosper the church in every one of those disciplines. "I will abundantly bless her provision; I will satisfy her poor with bread" (Psalm 132:15). The blessing of God satisfies because it is an abundant blessing. God's blessing is abundant because it is a spiritual blessing and it is an eternal blessing.

The abundant blessing of God has an ultimate source. God made a covenant which cannot be broken. "I will clothe her priests with salvation" (Psalm 132:16). Under the old covenant, the priest was the mediator between God and man. The priests were consecrated by ritual bathing, anointing and sacrifices. These symbolized cleansing and purity which was necessary to mediate between holy God and sinful man. The old covenant priests were types of the one true Mediator, the Lord Jesus Christ. He is "clothed with righteousness" (Psalm 132:9). The Lord Jesus Christ has ordained ministers to announce the abundant blessing to the people of God, *Coram Deo*. "And her saints shall shout aloud for joy" (Psalm 132:16).

Where is that joy in the worship services today? Has it been absconded by false doctrine, programs, entertainment or church managers? It may be a combination of all the above.

There was an internet survey about religion a few years ago that required objective responses. About fifty people responded to this question: Do you go to a church, temple, synagogue, mosque, or anything? Why or why not? Do you believe there is something greater than this world? What role does religion play in your life, if any? Negative respondents were a large majority. A couple of responses will suffice to make the point. "I despise organized religion; it bears far too many similarities to organized crime." To an unbeliever the organization and its building known as the "church" may conjure up criminal thoughts. If he was a believer, he never experienced joy in worship. One man said his denomination reminded him of a kinder, gentler KKK. A sad commentary indeed when the church reminds someone of terrorism. Another person said, "In 1989 I was 16 and went to a Youth for Christ camp, I gave my life to God....but a couple of years later I felt like a fake, I still didn't know who I was and really questioned God." He or she was probably so busy with evangelism, music ministry, fellowship, and other programs that he or she never experienced joy in worship.

Worship *Coram Deo* and experience joy in worship.

19. Worship is Like Heaven on Earth

Psalm 133

A brief review of the Psalms of Ascent will put this Psalm in the proper context. The Psalms of Ascent begin at Psalm 120 and end at Psalm 134. These Psalms describe the pattern, events, and expectations as the Old Testament congregation travelled to the temple of the living God located at Mount Zion to worship the true and living God. These Psalms of Ascent paint a beautiful picture as families move in the slow pace of a caravan toward the holy city of Jerusalem.

Psalm 120 describes a child of God who lives among unbelievers. The Bible describes those unbelievers in terms of hating peace and they want to engage in war. Psalm 124 describes the living conditions of the Old Testament saint. "When men rose up against us, then they would have swallowed us alive, when their wrath was kindled against us; then the waters would have overwhelmed us" (Psalm 124:2). In Psalm 129:2 the Psalmist says, "Many a time they have afflicted me from my youth." The Psalmist has described what it is like to live among unbelievers who hate the law of God. Furthermore unbelievers hate the children of God.

Christians also live in an unbelieving society, a rebellious and stubborn generation as the Bible describes it. They find the rebellious and stubborn generation in their work places, schools, social engagements and civic activities. Unbelievers are filled with unbelief, violence, hatred and bitterness.

These series of Psalms draw vivid pictures of travelling dangers and it reminds Christians of the dangers they face day to day in this unbelieving world. The enemy attacks them many ways. These Psalms also represent the faith, hope, and joy that God's children feel as they anticipate worship to the God of their salvation. These Psalms of Ascent teach Christians that God's providential care protects and strengthens them against the danger they face in a hostile and unbelieving world.

The beauty and splendor of the Temple was ever present in the mind of the pilgrim.

> I will lift up my eyes to the hills, from whence comes my help? My help comes from the Lord who made heaven and earth (Psalm 121:1).

> I was glad when they said to me, Let us go into the house of the Lord (Psalm 122:1).

> Unto You I will lift up my eyes, O You who dwell in the heavens (Psalm 123:1).

> Let us go into His tabernacle; Let us worship at His footstool (Psalm 132:7).

Christians should think like the Psalmist has written, because the unbelieving world cannot rob them of true worship to God. God's people find beauty and excellence in the temple of the Lord.

Psalm 133 is the climax of this series of Psalms of ascent. Only 40 Hebrew words in this Psalm, but what powerful words. This picture in Psalm 133 is that of the pilgrim having arrived in Jerusalem to see the House of God which is a far cry from the hostile and unbelieving world in Psalm 120. They are now in the presence of the Lord whom they love and serve. It is like Heaven on Earth!

Now before we look closer at this Psalm, please notice the first word in the Psalm. The *New International Version* excludes the first word, but it is in the Hebrew text. The first word in this Psalm is "behold." God used the word "behold" to get your attention. This interjection should provoke a sense of excitement.

It tells Christians to sit up, give attention, and listen to what God has to say.

"Behold, how good and pleasant it is for brethren to dwell together in unity!" The greatest joy in worship is to be in the presence of God. The next joy is to worship with brethren that are like-minded. Brethren ought to be understood in terms of the congregation of God's people. To live "together in unity" means to live according to God's Word.

The term "one anotherness" may best describe the manner in which Christians may understand unity among God's people. There are about two dozen of these "one another" commandments in the New Testament such as love one another, pray, forgive, teach one another, and so on.

In opposition to "one anotherness" is the "I am and there is no one else besides me" syndrome (Isaiah 47:10). It is the opposite of unity among the congregation of God's people. For example in Judges chapter twenty, brothers were killing each other. Unity presupposes relationships. Biblical "one anotherness" requires right relationships among Christians. Christians worship in unity because they have a right relationship; first to God and then among God's worshipers. It is like having Heaven on earth when Christians worship collectively with a sense of unity. Every Christian ought to examine himself or herself with these questions: Lord, am I obstructing the unity in this time of corporate collective worship? Am I offering worship that is not commanded in the Word of God?

The church collectively delights in unity; therefore Christians individually delight in each other. The church is the congregation of God's people called out for a special purpose. The church has the distinct privilege to gather together and worship the triune God. There must be unity among the many to have heaven on earth in worship. Behold, do you see heaven on earth when the church gathers for worship?

Behold the source of unity. "It is like the precious oil upon the head, running down on the beard, the beard of Aaron, running down on the edge of his garments" (Psalm133:2). The ritual of anointing the High Priest was symbolic of how God's blessing comes to his people. Aaron was set apart to act as the representative of God for all Israel and become the mediator between God and the sinful people of Israel.

The word picture describes the holy oil as it comes from above, down on Aaron's head and descends over his garments. The sacred oil flowed upon Aaron's richly adorned garments which contained the precious stones inscribed with the names of the twelve tribes of Israel, the *urim* and the *thummim*. The whole body was consecrated in all its parts. This vivid picture of the holy anointing oil describes the unity mentioned in verse one. The anointing comes from above, flowing to all the members so they all participate in the blessing. The anointing was a symbol of the presence of the Holy Spirit.

The blessing of God does not come through human institutions. The Old Testament symbolism is no longer necessary. The blessing of God's presence comes from heaven by the power of the Holy Spirit through the Mediator, the Lord Jesus Christ. Those who belong to Christ are blessed with all blessings in heavenly places (Ephesians 1:3). Christians know and experience the preciousness of unity, because they are in union with the blessing from God, the Lord Jesus Christ.

This Psalm also reveals the nature of the unity that Christians experience. "It is like the dew of Hermon, descending upon the mountains of Zion" (Psalm 133:3). This figure of speech describes the blessing of unity in terms of nature and geography. Hermon is a mountain located adjacent to Lebanon and is noted for its majesty, size and beauty. It is the highest mountain in Syria at 9200 feet above sea level. Zion, of course, is the much smaller mountain (2500 feet above sea level) where the Temple was located and to which the analogy is made in our text. The significance of Mount Zion to Mount Hermon in the mind of the Psalmist was its dew. When the air of the evening cooled the intense heat, the moisture condensed and fell upon the lower and dryer land. It was refreshing dew to the dry land in Palestine. Hermon is 100 miles north of Jerusalem, but there is a natural relationship in a supernatural way between the dew that falls on the lofty Hermon and the humbler Zion. The refreshing dew that belongs in another place is present with the pilgrim in Jerusalem. It is as if the thing that belongs in another place is present at another place. To use a simile that brings the beauty of the figure into focus, it is like having Heaven on Earth.

The nature of Christian unity is like the dew that drenches the parched ground, dew that refreshes and revives. There is suddenly in a supernatural way, a lushness and plenitude of God's grace being poured out to the soul. The dew from God's heavenly realm touches us as we have communion with the Lord Jesus Christ. The nature of this unity is found when God baptizes his people with his renewing and refreshing presence. The anointing of the Holy Spirit saturates the congregation of God's people. The dew from God's heavenly realm touches Christians as they have communion in unity with the Lord Jesus Christ.

At the end of a work day do you rejoice that you can spend some time alone with the Lord and worship with your family? Do you enjoy the beauty and presence of unity when you have private worship? What about when you gather your family together to worship? Is there a sense of closeness among the family? On the Lord's Sabbath Day, do you rejoice that you can worship with the family of God with the local church? Do you enjoy the beauty and presence of unity among God's children?

Those questions come in the face of daily burdens. The daily difficulties and doubts may confuse the Christian who just days before experienced joy in worship. Strife and disturbed relationships may seem to overwhelm Christians. During those times remember that "the Lord commanded the blessing – Life forevermore" (Psalm 133:3). Trials, temptations, and suffering are temporary. Remember God's blessing. Your burdens will be lifted, your doubts cast aside, and strife will turn into spiritual understanding. Remember how good and pleasant is was to worship together in unity. It will last forever in the New Heavens and the New Earth.

There are three ways to preserve unity and have Heaven on Earth.

    1. Worship the Lord privately.
    2. Father's lead their families in worship.
    3. God's covenant people gather for the special blessing God each Sabbath day.

The Lord has ordered the blessing of unity to fall on his people, who are united together to worship the true and living God, so they can experience Heaven on Earth.

20. Double Blessing in Worship

Psalm 134

Esau returned from a hunting trip and learned that Jacob came deceitfully and had taken away Esau's blessing.

> And Esau said, 'Is he not rightly named Jacob? For he has supplanted me these two times. He took away my birthright, and now look, he has taken away my blessing!' And he said, 'have you not reserved a blessing for me?' Then Isaac answered and said to Esau, 'Indeed I have made him our master, and all his brethren I have given to him as servants with grain and wine I have sustained him. What shall I do now for you, my son?' And Esau said to his father, "have you only one blessing, my father? Bless me – me also my father!' And Esau lifted up his voice and wept. Genesis 27:36-38).

Esau hated Jacob and threatened to kill him. The blessing is to be desired, so much that Esau wept when he lost his father's blessing. Rather than Isaac pronouncing Esau the head of the family, Jacob was announced the head of the family. What is this blessing that a man is willing to lie to receive it and even risk death?

The blessing in the Old Testament intends to convey a gift by a pronouncement. We find it early in the Bible. For instance, God blessed the creation (Genesis 1:22). The divine blessing represents God's presence expressing His goodness. It must be remembered that the divine blessing is more *kairotic* than *chronologic.* God's blessing will have a lasting effect, but the pronouncement has a heightened awareness of God's presence. God's blessing is more spiritual than material.

When man blesses God it is in reference to praise and thanksgiving. The people of God were told "Stand up and bless the Lord your God forever and ever! Blessed be Your glorious name, which is exalted above all blessing and praise" (Nehemiah 9:5).

The last of the pilgrim Psalms refers to a "double blessing in worship." It captures the scene of the final hours of worship on that particular occasion. The inspired Word of God begins this Psalm with the word "Behold." Your attention is being commanded. Listen to the words and draw a mental image of this special event. This text describes the Old Testament worshiper during the final hours before his long trip back home.

Behold, is also applicable for the New Testament worshiper because it tells you to pay attention to this Psalm, think and meditate on the picture it paints as you assemble to worship. The Lord Jesus Christ has given you a blessing far greater than the Old Testament saint.

Behold the context of this Psalm. The people are gathered for the last time before they leave on the long trip home. The activities of the day were emotionally charged. They had said to each other, "how good and how pleasant it is for brethren to dwell in together in unity." They were aware that the peace they had experienced over the past few days would soon end and war would be on minds of the unbelievers with whom they lived and worked. They worshipped among brethren who wanted peace and unity, but they worked among unbelievers who wanted to fight, argue, and dispute. During that day many were beginning to share the farewell hugs and final words to those they love in the faith.

As the day comes to a close and they anticipate leaving early on the next day the worshipers commend the ministers of the Lord to continue their exercise of public ministry. The worshiper doesn't intend to stop worshiping when he or she leaves Jerusalem. The worshiper took serious the injunction of the Ten Commandments summarized in these few words: "Love the Lord your God with all your heart, with all your soul and with all your strength" (Deuteronomy 6:5), and "love your neighbor as yourself" (Leviticus 19:18).

Worship to the Lord never ends, but the public gathering of God's people for worship will be interrupted for a short period of time. The covenant people expect the ministers of the Lord to continue praying and praising God until they gather in public worship again.

The Levites were the servants of the Lord. They had been ordained to the ministry so they might engage the Old Testament saint in public worship. As servants of the Lord they had the responsibility of leading God's people in worship. The Old Testament worshiper expected the Levites to bless God. The Levites were ministers and were charged to speak well of God. If the Levites obeyed God's plan for worship, the public worship of God should bring God's people into a state of blessedness.

Today, ministers of the Lord are more interested in building empires than serving as ministers before the Lord. I've heard all the defenses of the monstrous ministries in this country, but I am neither convinced by Scripture or necessary inference that worship can be electronically functional. Worship, like the pastoral ministry, is personal relative. Worship necessitates ascribing worth to God according to His regulative principle in Scripture. The minister leads the congregation in worship.

The minister ought to devote himself to the service of leading God's people in worship. Godly biblical worship has been fractured because too many ministers have rejected the concept of being a "servant to the Lord" and replaced it with being a servant to the people. The Lord Jesus left His church with a clear understanding of the servant of God.

> Whoever desires to become great among you, let him be your servant. And whoever desires to be first among you, let him be your slave – just as the Son of Man did not

come to be served, but to serve, and to give His life a ransom for many. (Matthew 20:26-28)

As it was in the days of Jesus, the apostle Paul and throughout the history of the church, the greatest majority of professing Christians despise servant hood. The biblical terminology for servant hood is slave or bondservant; it means that one serves in bondage to another.

We must not try to hide the meaning of the words of Scripture, so that the words become meaningless. The apostle Paul was a man who had been given authority by Jesus Christ to serve as a minister in His church. It is for that reason that Paul was compelled to serve the church at Corinth. In the truest sense of the word a minister of Jesus Christ is a servant to the church. It logically follows then that every Christian is a minister, because the Bible commands Christians to serve one another (Galatians 5:13). It could be translated "minister ye as slaves to one another." The character of a true minister is one who serves.

God calls some among the ministers to serve as a pastor. It is his duty to lead God's people in worship according to the Word of God. Although the minister must pronounce the blessing in worship, he must not forget that he must be a blessing. The apostle Paul told Timothy to "be an example to the believers in word, in conduct, in love, in spirit, in faith, in purity" (1 Timothy 4:12).

The servant of the Lord in relation to Old Testament Temple worship was the Levite. We find specific instructions for these servants in Numbers 3:5ff. The Levites service was 24 hours a day as "they were employed in that service day and night" (1 Chronicles 9:33). They were to guard the holy things of the Temple with diligence. I expect there were un-ordained men who stayed with the Levites throughout the night. Luke tells us that Anna did not depart from the Temple day or night. We need some Anna's today. While the congregation was sleeping the priests were guarding the temple. It was their business to carry out their ministerial duties as they are needed both day and night.

The servants of the Lord were told to lift up their hands toward the temple. I take it that the temple servants were in the temple court thus raising their hands toward the temple because it was the dwelling place of God on earth. The duties of the servants and the expectations of the worshipers are the corpus of this final Psalm of Ascent.

The scope and end of corporate public collective worship is the blessedness of God. The announcement and interest in God's goodness is the first and last thought in worship. The first thought and duty of the temple servant, now known as the minister, is to lead the worshiper to "bless the Lord." "Behold, bless the Lord, all you servants of the Lord, who by night stand in the house of the Lord! Lift up your hands in the sanctuary, and bless the Lord" (Psalm 134:1-2). The worshiper blesses the Lord by offering praise and thanksgiving to the Lord who made heaven and earth. This kind of blessing from the worshiper will continue throughout eternity (Revelation 5:11). The lifting up of hands by the worshiper is the visible expression of praise and thanksgiving.

The congregation of God's people will bless the Lord with exhilarating joy if the many worship in unity.

> The many pray in unity.
> The many confess in unity.
> The many agree with the Word of God in unity.
> The many sing Psalms and hymns in unity.
> The many bless the Lord in unity.

To put this into theological perspective, the unity of the plurality pronounces the goodness of God as the final measure of praise and adoration.

Worship is the center of God's covenantal design. Post fall man knows very well that in God's covenant relationship there is a blessing for obedience and a curse for disobedience. So it is in worship. Christians bless the Lord according to His regulative principle. For being obedient to His Word, the Lord blesses His children from Zion (Psalm 134:3).

The men in unity bless the Lord and the Lord in unity blesses the many. The heart and soul passion of Christians is to bless the Lord and to receive the Lord's blessing.

The blessing of God's covenant perfections and His excellencies is the blessing Christians expect out of Zion. Then there is the blessing of being in communion with God, through the Mediator, the Lord Jesus Christ, by the power of the Holy Spirit.

The Lord Jesus Christ came so Christians might have a Mediator that made the final sacrifice for their souls. He is the Mediator that gives the people of God the privilege and duty to lift up hands, heart, mind and all that is in you to worship the triune God of heaven and earth anytime and anyplace.

It's time to get up. We have to make that long trip back home. We will descend from Zion and go back to Mesheck. We must return home, but we've been blessed by the Lord who made heaven and earth. We have been blessed with life evermore. The Lord will bless you from His dwelling place. We have experienced joy in worship!

21. How to Offer Perfect Worship

Hebrews 7:26-28

Many Christians do not believe there is a perfect church, therefore perfect worship is not possible. There is a perfect church. It is called the triumphant church or sometimes referred to as the invisible church. The term "invisible church" does not mean that no one can see the invisible church. Webster's Dictionary defines invisible as "incapable of being seen" or "not presently apparent." The latter definition is applicable to the concept of the invisible church. The triune God, the angels and all the saints in heaven can see the invisible church. It is a mistake to call the true church merely transcendental. Properly it is the invisible church, the church that God sees in its perfected form. The perfect church is in heaven receiving all those whose names are written in "the Lamb's Book of Life" (Revelation 21:27). The eternal Sabbath is the perfection of all worship.

The church on earth is not perfect, however perfect worship is not only possible, it is necessary. This is not an argument for a perfect church. Despair must not overtake the saints of God. There always has been and always will be local congregations that worship God according to His will. However, it is impossible for a saved sinner to offer perfect worship. There must be a remedy for the paradox. Martin Murphy explains the crux of the problem.

> Human beings are worshiping creatures, therefore they are religious people. Human beings were created to worship God, but because of the fall they worship the creature rather than the Creator. The history of the human race is a history of worshiping people. The apostle Paul addressed the philosophers at Athens. It was a place and a people especially given to intellectual stimulation and

with it the high culture of the day. Upon arriving in the arena, Paul "stood up in the meeting of the Areopagus" and brought up some of the observations of his tour of Athens. "Men of Athens! I see that in every way you are very religious. For as I walked around and looked carefully at your objects to worship, I even found an altar with this inscription: TO AN UNKNOWN GOD" (*The Essence of Christian Doctrine*, by Martin Murphy, p. 137).

God not only demands worship, His creatures are wired for worship. The twist is that God requires perfect worship and sinners are incapable of perfection. The answer to the dilemma is to have someone perfect to intercede for saved sinners. The Mediator, the Lord Jesus Christ, is that person. "We have such a High Priest, who is seated at the right hand of the throne of the Majesty in the heavens, a Minister of the sanctuary and of the true tabernacle which the Lord erected, and not man" (Hebrews 8:1-2). Jesus Christ the great high Priest intercedes for all of those God calls to be children of God. "For such a High Priest was fitting for us, who is holy, harmless, undefiled, separate from sinners, and has become higher than the heavens; who does not need daily, as those high priests, to offer up sacrifices, for His own sins and then for the people's for this He did once for all when He offered up Himself" (Hebrews 7:26-28).

The saved sinner still has a sinful nature. The problem is not just sin, but the result of sin itself. Justification removes the guilt, but the corruption remains (Romans 7:19; James 3:2). When Christians pray, worship, and live *Coram Deo*, they must have a High Priest that is without sin. Christians ought to find great comfort that the perfect High Priest appears before God as spokesman and representative of God's people. As the great High Priest, the Lord Jesus Christ brings men into the presence of God. Worship offered through the perfect Mediator, the Lord

Jesus Christ, according to the Word of God is perfect worship in the presence of God.

This biblical principle that requires Christ the Mediator also requires Christ the Savior. Is there an uncomfortable feeling about this whole concept? If the Word of God requires worship offered through the Lord Jesus, then the worshiper must have the Christ as Savior. If Christ is the Savior, He is also the Lord. If Jesus Christ is the second person of the Trinity, then He is the great High Priest. If He is the High Priest and the Minister in the heavenly sanctuary, then He is the Mediator. If this is all true, then the evangelical church is faced with a serious dilemma. Should unbelievers be invited to a worship service? If so why? If the answer is "to be saved" that is not the purpose of a worship service. The ministry of evangelism ought to precede an invitation to worship.

Eighteenth century Revivalism in this country introduced a new concept that was eventually incorporated into public worship. Many evangelicals participate in this new apparition now known as the invitation during worship to God. The invitation system originated during the time that evangelistic meetings were held for the proclamation of the good news of the kingdom of Jesus Christ. Itinerant preachers conducted camp meetings with the sole purpose to convince unbelievers to trust Christ for salvation. The church historian, Kenneth Scott Latourette, describes the 18th century revival meetings.

> The custom of camp-meetings spread and persisted. Hundreds, sometimes thousands, flocked to a camp ground, many from curiosity or as a social gathering in a new country where opportunities for large concourses of people were rare. The emotional and physical accompaniments were often extreme and bizarre (*A History of Christianity*, vol. 2, p. 1037, by Kenneth Scott Latourette)

What began as an evangelistic meeting for the conversion of lost souls, eventually turned into a worship service for the conversion of the lost. How did this happen? The expansion of the evangelical church during the 18th and 19th centuries took place without consulting the full counsel of God. In part it was due to the lack of theological education in the rapidly growing church. The modern church was also influenced by pragmatism, the church growth movement and the seeker sensitivity philosophy. Custom came to dominate the ministry of the church rather that biblical and theological mandates. Dr. Harold M. Parker, Jr., a church historian, explains how the church and its leaders erred.

> [The] error lies in the tendency for the student to follow the authority ahead of him in Indian file, deeper and deeper into the morass of error. If the first of the secondary authorities is wrong in fact or judgment, then all who follow him will be in error also, for they are on the same path. They will remain in error until the primary sources are checked again. (*Studies in Southern Presbyterian History*, by Harold M. Parker, Jr., p. 56)

Ad fontes; it is time to consult the primary source – the Word of God. Jesus said, "Go therefore and make disciples of all the nations...teaching them to observe all things that I have commanded you; and lo, I am with you always, even to the end of the age" (Matthew 28:19-20).

Making disciples involves apologetics, evangelism, and teaching the Word of God. God does not command His church to worship Him with apologetics, evangelism, or teaching. If a particular church has on-going evangelistic efforts, there ought to be regular evangelistic meetings where unbelievers are presented with the clear gospel message and an opportunity to trust Christ. If there is a high resistance to the gospel message, Christian apologetics ought to be the order of the day. Unbelievers who make public professions of faith ought to be taught the Word of God by spiritually and doctrinally mature leaders in the church. Then the whole church consisting of those who trust Christ ought to gather in unity to offer worship to the triune God. Then they have the same Savior and Lord and the same Word of God to direct them in worship.

The Lord Jesus Christ said, "I must preach the kingdom of God to the other cities also, because for this purpose I have been sent" (Luke 4:43). The verb "sent" translates from the Greek word *apostello*. The mission of making disciples requires authority from the sender. Therefore, Christ gives His disciples authority to carry out the great evangelistic enterprise (Matthew 28:17-20). If you trust Christ as your Lord and Savior, then you are His disciple. Every individual Christian is an emissary with authority to announce the gospel message. Those who refuse to trust Christ do not have the perfect interceding Mediator to offer worship to God.

Believers have the Lord Jesus Christ as Mediator who intercedes for them. The Bible assures Christians that "He always lives to make intercession for them" (Hebrews 7:25). Christ is at the right hand of God making intercession for the saved sinner. The intercession of Christ mentioned in the Bible includes more than prayer and salvation. Francis Turretin considered the full counsel of God to determine the meaning of Christ's intercession for the saints. "The offering of our persons and the sanctification of our prayers and of our entire worship, inasmuch as he presents all our prayers to God as spiritual sacrifices, perfumed with the most fragrant odor of his own sacrifice, so that in and through him they may be pleasing and acceptable to God" (*Institutes of Elenctic Theology*, vol. 2, page 485). Turretin concludes that "believers neither rely upon their own merit, nor seek nor obtain anything by and on account of themselves, but only in the name of Christ. Nor do they dare approach immediately to God without Christ…" The apostle Paul clarifies any misunderstanding. "It is Christ who died and furthermore is also risen, who is even at the right hand of God, who also makes intercession for us" (Romans 8:34). Believers ought to find joy in worship because their great High Priest, the Lord Jesus Christ, is on His eternal throne interceding so that their worship is perfected, *Coram Deo*.

22. The Benediction

Numbers 6:22-27

Mrs. Church Goer leans over and whispers to Mr. Church Goer "get out your car keys, he is about to announce the benediction." For many church goers the benediction is the signal that everything is about over. It is time to go home. If that is the way professing Christians think, apparently worship does not stimulate their senses and awareness of being in the presence of God. It should. Otherwise they may not be worshiping the true and living God. The benediction is not the end of worship, but the fulfillment of joy in worship.

The benediction, from the Latin word *benedictio*, means "blessing." It is a pronouncement of God's blessing upon his people. Christians should recognize the benediction as biblical. While the practice of pronouncing blessings goes as far back as Melchizedek to Abraham (Gen 14.18-20), Isaac to Jacob (Gen 27.26-29), and Jacob to his sons (Gen 48-49), the primary source is that of the Aaronic blessing found in Numbers 6.22-27.

The world is full of chaos and confusion. It used to be that adults murdered adults. Now children are killing each other. Adults acting like children. We live in a nation pilfering its citizens. Some churches despise the doctrine of Christ; even some evangelical churches prefer unity at any cost. Many frown on the sound teaching of Scripture. What is the reason for this kind of behavior? There is a subliminal desire for cosmic harmony. Chaos is the opposite of cosmos. Chaos is disorder and cosmos is order. Confusion is the opposite clarity. Confusion is the brother of chaos.

Christians cannot escape this chaos and confusion, because they live in this sinful world. Sooner or later professing Christians get accustomed to the chaos and confusion and opt to overlook it, try to ignore it, or simply get used to it. The chaos and confusion is still there and there are times when it emerges with great fury, but most of the time they suppress it and go about their business. Who knows, maybe one day it will go away?

Every fashionable aberration known to man including all presumed psychological, sociological, or philosophical discoveries set the agenda to sooth the pain and hurt that comes from chaos and confusion, however none of them bring order and harmony to the reality of life.

One reason Christians want to gather and worship God together is with the hope of escaping the confusion and chaos in the world. All too often the expectations are short lived because worship may be chaotic and confusing.

Christian ought to ask themselves this heart searching question. Is the motive for assembling for worship the glory of God or has the glory of God in worship been abandoned for the sake of evangelism, revivalism, moralism, or some other man-made religious performance?

Some Christians may be so hardened to the chaos and confusion in this life that worship on the Lord's Day does not find its proper place in the heart. True worship according to God's desire will bring joy. It is pure joy to bless the Lord in worship by singing Psalms and hymns, prayer to Him and about Him, reading and preaching the Word of God, administrating the ordinances of God according to His Word, and receiving God's blessing in the benediction.

The glory of God's benediction in worship is God's response to His church. It is exceedingly great joy for God to bless His people in worship. There is a sense in which the benediction is the most important part of the worship service. It is the primary part of worship that actually helps Christians deal with the chaos and confusion that they face day after day.

Do Christians think the benediction is a benevolent prophecy? To put it another way do Christians think that for the next week they expect good things to happen. Does that mean they will have a happy life? Happiness is the meaning of God's

The Benediction

blessing for many professing Christians. If Christians think in materialistic terms, the blessing of God means plenty of material things and lots of happiness.

However, God's benediction has nothing to do with material things or even your happiness for that matter. The benediction in worship is a blessing pronounced by God's minister for the people of God. The nature of God's blessing is often misunderstood. The watershed effect of such thinking has distorted the biblical doctrine of worship.

The inspired apostle Paul announced the benediction to God's people at the close of many of his letters to the churches. He employed different words, but the essence of his benedictions are the same. The benediction Paul used in His inspired letter to the Ephesians is particularly comforting because it is from God the Father and the Lord Jesus Christ (Ephesians 6:23-24). Paul sent a minister so that the Ephesians may know the glory of God's church and to be encouraged by the good news of God's glory (Ephesians 6:21-22).

God's benediction announces His peace, faith, and love (Ephesians 6:23). Peace, love, and faith are gifts from God. Christians realize these gifts through the Lord Jesus Christ, because He is the Mediator of all spiritual blessings. God has given his people peace. First, they have peace with God through the Lord Jesus Christ. Then what naturally follows is peace with God's children as they join together for worship. Peace is a state of being. Peace is not something that Christians deserve and they are incapable of earning it. Peace is a gift from God. Peace is not co-mingled with chaos and confusion.

Collective worship according to God's desire is the zenith of all human experience. The benediction is the summit of Christian worship. The glory of God is manifest in His benediction. God's blessing uniquely brings us before His face.

God's instruments of comfort for the heart are the faithful ministers in the Lord. God appointed those faithful ministers to announce His benediction. The symbolism of the minister lifting his hands or in some cases the lifting of the right hand is symbolical. The lifting of the hands by the minster, not the congregation, represents the sovereign God in the highest heavens blessing His subjects in their state of humility. God's hands are above His people as they bow in reverence and humility. In Leviticus 9.22, "Aaron lifted up his hands toward the people and blessed them." The lifting of the hands of the benefactor is gloriously evident when Jesus "led them out as far as Bethany, and lifting up his hands he blessed them" (Luke 24:50-51). The lifting up of the hands should remind Christians that the blessing from God comes from above. It is the spiritual nature of the benediction that brings the Christian worshiper to the realization that the chaos and confusion in life is temporal.

The reason for the chaos and confusion in the Christian life is because of the instability and lack of confidence Christians have in reality. They seek satisfaction in the things of this world rather than the things that belong to God in the spiritual world.

For instance, how many sermons have you heard on the beatific vision of God? In his book, *Theological Terms in Layman Language,* Martin Murphy explains the beatific vision. "The great hope of all believers, that in heaven we will see God as He is. Although theologians do not agree on the means to the end, this is the final destination of God's elect (Acts 7:56)." Another Latin term used by medieval theologians was the *visio Dei*. It literally means the appearance of God or to see God as He really is. To see the fullness of God is the desire of all human beings, especially Christian human beings.

Just think of how God revealed Himself to Moses in the burning bush, at the Red Sea opening, and miraculously furnished food. After these spectacular revelations, Moses was not satisfied. Moses pleaded with God saying, "please show me your glory." God said to Moses, "I will put you in the cleft of the rock, and will cover you with My hand while I pass by. Then I will take away My hand, and you shall see My back, but My face shall not be seen" (Exodus 33:18-23). No man can see the face

The Benediction

of God and live. People want to see a physical image of God, but it is not possible, so they try to fill that void with thousands of idols, thoughts, and ideas. Christians ought to desire the beatific vision of God. If preachers would spend more time preaching on the beatific vision, Christian worshipers may see the glory of God in His benediction in a fuller more complete sense.

In the absence of seeing God's face or even the absence of *theophanies* (the burning bush) God prescribed a benediction to be announced by God's minister to the congregation of God's people. We find the clearest prescription for God's benediction in Numbers 6:22-26. This is typical Hebrew parallelism. The same thought is conveyed in a different way in each individual stanza.

> The Lord bless you
> The Lord make his face shine upon you
> The Lord lift His countenance upon you
> The Lord keep you
> The Lord be gracious to you
> The Lord give you peace.

God's presence and peace with Him will bring harmony and order to your life. God invites his people into His presence in a collective worship service on the Lord's Day. They should take great pleasure in godly worship. The time of collective worship is not an entertainment theater. Worship does not have man in mind. True worship is God-centered. God brings His children into His presence, gives them His peace, and sends them away with His benediction.

All the intellectual and emotional capacities should be exercised when Christians humbly receive the benediction. The inspired benediction to the church at Ephesus was "Grace be with all those who love our Lord Jesus Christ in sincerity" (Ephesians 6:24). Grace marks God's benediction to God's people who love the Lord Jesus Christ with imperishable love.

There is a sense in which God's benediction marks the elect so that they will not be led astray by the lies of this world which are so often found in chaos and confusion. "We should no longer be children, tossed to and fro and carried about with every wind of doctrine, by the trickery of men, in the cunning craftiness of deceitful plotting" (Ephesians 4:14). If professing Christians do not heed the warning, the result is devastating. Paul referred to the Gentiles (those who do not have Jesus as Lord and Savior) as being alienated from God (Ephesians 4:18). Alienation from God brings chaos and confusion to its maximum effect. In the end those will be cut off from God's benediction.

If you are not in a favorable relationship with God, pray that the Holy Spirit will change your heart. Seek the Lord while he may be found. Believe on the Lord Jesus Christ so you will have peace with God.

The benediction is for those who have peace with God and love with faith. The blessing will be the very presence of God. Grace is the promise for all those who love the Lord Jesus Christ with an incorruptible love.

As ambassadors of Christ, Christians ought to receive God's benediction. Then go into the world to call unbelievers to faith in Jesus Christ, because it is the blood of Christ that makes the benediction possible.

About the Author

Pastor James Vickery is a builder and servant of the Lord. He began to pastor God's people at an early age and for years has sought to encourage, edify and build the kingdom of God. Those that know him can attest to his dedication and efforts to grow and bless the work of the Lord. Except for the time he took to further his education, he constantly served as a pastor. Whether he had to work a secular job and pastor or just pastor, he has been faithful to the call he received at a young age.

www.ingramcontent.com/pod-product-compliance
Lightning Source LLC
LaVergne TN
LVHW051101080426
835508LV00019B/2007